Teaching Religion and Science

D0076122

Can religion and science co-exist successfully in the classroom?

How can you encourage an environment where differing views are treated positively?

How do you help students apply their understanding of religious beliefs and scientific theory to a range of ultimate questions?

Teaching Religion and Science aims to give religious education teachers a pedagogical foundation for the teaching of religion and science topics, and for the teaching of religion as a whole. It will help you to have the confidence to include what might appear to be challenging or controversial topics in your lessons, and provides guidance on how religion and science themes can be effectively addressed using appropriate classroom teaching methods.

Containing a wealth of practical advice to help you turn pedagogical theory into practice effortlessly, it helps you understand your own attitudes to the subject, as well as those of your students, to ensure successful teaching. Essential guidance includes:

- activities to help you apply pedagogic practices to your own particular classroom situation
- advice to help minimize potential difficulties whilst tackling controversial issues
- links to a wide range of resources and advice on further reading
- comprehensive lesson plans for ages 11–16 and 16–19.

Designed to be a resource for all training and practising RE teachers, *Teaching Religion and Science* offers much-needed support for successfully integrating the teaching of religion and science in your classroom.

Tonie Stolberg is Lecturer in Science and Science Education at the University of Birmingham, UK.

Geoff Teece is Lecturer in Religious Education and Director of Studies for Initial Teacher Education at the University of Birmingham, UK.

Teaching Religion and Science

Effective pedagogy and practical approaches for RE teachers

Tonie Stolberg and Geoff Teece

Routledge
Taylor & Francis Group

LONDON AND NEW YORK

First published 2011
by Routledge
2 Park Square, Milton Park, Abingdon, Oxon, OX14 4RN

Simultaneously published in the USA and Canada
by Routledge
270 Madison Avenue, New York, NY 10016

Routledge is an imprint of the Taylor & Francis Group, an informa business

© 2011 Tonie Stolberg and Geoff Teece

Typeset in Bembo by Pindar NZ, Auckland, New Zealand
Printed and bound in Great Britain by TJ International Ltd,
Padstow, Cornwall

British Library Cataloguing in Publication Data
A catalogue record for this book is available from the British
Library

Library of Congress Cataloging-in-Publication Data
Stolberg, Tonie.
Teaching religion and science : effective pedagogy and practical
approaches for RE teachers / Tonie Stolberg and Geoff Teece.
— 1st ed.
    p. cm.
   1. Religion— Study and teaching 2. Science— Study and
teaching 3. Religion and science— Study and teaching. I. Teece,
Geoff. II. Title.
  BL41.S68 2011
  201'.6507— dc22   2010006915

ISBN13: 978–0–415–54819–9 (hbk)
ISBN13: 978–0–415–54820–5 (pbk)
ISBN13: 978–0–203–84543–1 (ebk)

Contents

Acknowledgements

We would like to express our thanks for the enthusiasm and interest shown to our ideas by teachers and educators, and Mark for his review of an earlier draft of the book. We would especially like to extend our heartfelt gratitude to Jill for her encouragement, sensitivity and perseverance when asked to comment on our work in progress.

Chapter 1

Introduction

What this book is about

One of the greatest challenges for you, the teacher of religious education, is to develop successful ways of helping your students apply their understanding of religious beliefs and practices when exploring a range of ultimate questions, and moral and ethical issues. This book will outline a pedagogical approach to allow you to effectively address these objectives in your teaching and, at the same time, try to convince you that one of the means available to you in achieving these objectives is to effectively utilize the experience and opportunities gained by exploring the connections between religion and science.

The first part of this book focuses on two particular ways of thinking: the religious and the scientific, which are central to many an individual's – both the teacher's and their students' – ways of making sense of the world. The way we make sense of our physical being and environment has a direct impact on the teaching and learning of religious education. Since the examination of socio-scientific issues is a part of many religious education curricula, you and your students will need to understand how you view the natural world, and, therefore, in Chapter 2 we discuss the differences in approach of teachers and their students to understanding science's role in our lives and the possible underlying reasons for these variations.

The teaching of religion and science topics is often perceived to be controversial and difficult, unnecessary or even, for some, unwarranted and objectionable! In Chapter 3 we look at what it may be about our attitudes to religion and science that make it such a potentially challenging area to explore. We examine ways that will help you recognize and reflect on your own attitudes, enabling you to appreciate the many and varied viewpoints of your students – which may be divergent and different from your own – and the possible implications for your own approach to teaching.

In Chapter 4 we detail the pedagogical approach that informs the strategy and structure of the exemplar lessons described in Part 2. In this chapter, we look at how religious education teaching strategies can best grow and emerge from an understanding of the pedagogical approach within which you are working. We then describe a pedagogy, based on a clear appreciation of what is actually meant by phenomenological religious education, that is an effective way of engaging with religion and science issues within religious education curriculum.

In the second part of this book we then look at our suggestions as to how you might put this pedagogical approach into practice. In Chapter 5, we explain how the teaching of science and religious topics might best be approached, and a 'skilful' teaching strategy that will help you to do it.

Chapter 6 deals with the specific issues surrounding the teaching of topics that might be perceived as 'controversial', and therefore may cause particular challenges for both yourself and your students. We also detail some 'ground rules' that should minimize some of the potential difficulties you might encounter during your teaching.

The remaining chapters put the pedagogic advice previously described into practice: Chapter 7 details the planning and teaching content of religious education lessons for students aged 11–16 and Chapter 8 for ages 16–19. As curricula will vary significantly between countries and fluctuate from school to school, the lessons described are not intended to be units that can be 'slotted in' to your school planning, it should, however, be easy to adapt or extend the lessons to suit your particular situation.

What this book is *not* about

An unusual focus perhaps, but we feel we must be clear and address what some readers might suspect to be this book's 'hidden' motives. First, we are not in any way wishing to encourage the adoption of a religious world view – be it Christian or otherwise – as the best or appropriate means of making sense of the physical world we inhabit. We have tried to make a useful resource for religious education teachers who have a strong, personal religious faith, for teachers who would not wish to align themselves with any particular religious outlook, but also for those teachers who see a humanistic approach as the best way to understand themselves and others.

Second, the pedagogical approach we endorse is not designed to promote Christianity, or any other set of religious values. We feel that the teaching approach expounded upon in this book is equally applicable to learning about and from religion in countries in which there is a clear legislative distinction between the promotion of religion and the education of the citizen, as well as in those countries – including the country in which we, the authors, work – that allow schools to have a clear and distinctive religious mission as part of their educational identity. What is certain is that no matter the curriculum conditions within which you teach, you will have classes of students with a diverse range of views on religious belief and its relevance *to them* – even if they are drawn from what appears to be a seemingly mono-cultural community.

Finally, this book is not aimed at the teachers or the teaching of any other subjects. If you think your colleagues from other faculties would gain from the approach and ideas we outline then, we would, of course, not wish to discourage collaboration and co-operation. The content, however, is specifically focused on showing how you, the religious education teacher, might make best use of ideas, information and issues which draw their insights from an exploration of the physical world.

What this book will help you to do

The UK is unusual in that state schools do not adopt a faith-based confessional approach to the teaching of religious education. Nevertheless, how the teaching of religion should be undertaken in schools has become a source of disagreement and controversy.

In the 1970s, the influential work of Ninian Smart saw the development of what has come to be known as the phenomenological approach to religious education. Its proponents see it as the only way an education system can effectively help prepare its students to engage with the plurality of religions individual children will meet in their daily lives and the wide range of faiths they will encounter in their religious studies. Its critics, however, claim that students end up obtaining an understanding of religions that is uncritical and relativistic. In Chapter 4 we look in detail at the issues surrounding the teaching of religious education and explain how such criticisms might be addressed.

What is not disputed, however, is that a clear pedagogical strategy helps teachers in addressing the complex issue of effectively teaching religious education to classes consisting of students with a diverse range of faith positions. Frequently, teachers have to wrestle with the problem of reconciling their own religious (or non-religious) commitments with the variety of perspectives they are expected to teach. This especially comes to the fore when they find themselves required to deal with controversial ethical issues that may arise from the claims and practices of specific religions. Equally, students have to be assisted as they re-examine their own commitments in the light of the range of points of view they encounter in such courses.

Your students need to be encouraged to develop an open attitude to new discoveries and experiences, and interact positively with differing views rather than see them as threats to their own position. To do this, this book will give you a teaching approach that helps your students to understand the position they take within their tradition and then to evaluate their relationship to their tradition by engaging with the ongoing arguments within that tradition, and the conflicts it has with other systems of thought.

There is, however, also the possibility that, once they have exhausted the argumentative resources within a particular tradition, a student may find that they do not have the necessary concepts to uphold their particular point of view. So, this book also suggests an approach to the teaching and understanding of religions that would allow your students to develop a sense of personal transcendence – the opportunity to move beyond a particular state of knowledge and awareness to a broader and deeper knowledge and perspective.

The place of religion and science in the religious education curriculum

Recent years have seen dramatic developments in, what we might call, the 'intended' curriculum for the teaching of religious education in English secondary schools. The recently published Programmes of Study for religious education in England and the 2004 *Non-Statutory National Framework for Religious Education* (National Framework for RE) upon which they are based, focus on the study of Christianity and other principal religions, how religion and belief impact on individuals, families, the community and a secular world view, and, as part of a wider approach, how all can be taught through religion and science by examining the thematic issues of truth, explanation, meaning and purpose.

The pedagogical approach to teaching religious education that we propose explicitly demands the integration of the teaching of religion and science into the religious education curriculum. An examination of the teaching units in Chapters 7 and 8 will quickly show that effective teaching and learning of religious education *through* the study of religion and science requires that they are interwoven with the other themes outlined in the National Framework. These are, namely, the teaching of religious education through: an analysis of religious beliefs, concepts and notions of authority. How and why an understanding of the self and human experiences is expressed in a variety of forms. The questions and influences that inform our ethical and moral choices, what religions and beliefs say about human rights and responsibilities and the study of relationships, conflicts and collaboration within and between religions and beliefs.

Useful sources

There are, of course, numerous magazines, websites, television programmes, books, organizations and fora that explore the relationships between scientific and religious ideas, explanations and practices. Many of these examine a particular religious teaching or approach, or look at a specific scientific phenomena or theoretical perspective. There are also many writers that seek to describe – almost invariably from a particular, religious, philosophical or methodological perspective – the anthropological, historical, societal, cultural, psychological, neurological, physiological or, when thought appropriate, spiritual relationships between scientific and religious habits of mind. We urge you to explore and examine the diversity of perspectives that exist. We, of course, assume that you are most likely to focus on those writers that chime with your own assumptions so, at the end of this and each chapter, we have indicated what we feel are useful readings and organizations that might help you to look at your own assumptions (there is more on this in the next chapter) and those of your students.

There are also a growing number of resources aimed at both the teacher and their students that explore religion and science issues. Again, many are produced by organizations or individuals who have an agenda, which means that the range and content of the material presented could be skewed, biased or even misleading. We are not suggesting that this material should never be used, but you should make yourself aware of a lesson activity's origins, try not to rely on one particular source for your lesson content – sometimes, however, you will wish to consciously focus on a particular religious or philosophical perspective to illustrate a particular teaching point – and, where necessary, look at how the same topic is addressed by different products. Again, we have indicated what we feel are useful sources that might enable you to develop lesson content that is appropriate for your situation.

Please note, the choice of sources listed here, or in the rest of the book, should not in any way be taken as an indication of our own particular personal viewpoints, but may well indicate our ignorance of what is available! Also, even though the author's perspective and the 'limitations' of each resource are often obvious, we would recommend that you make yourself aware of these before using a particular resource in the classroom.

Here we list some of the sources that focus on a broad sweep of religion and science issues:

Further reading

Astley, J. Brown, D. and Loades, A. (eds) (2004) *Problems in Theology 4: Science and Religion*. London: T & T Clark.

This reader brings together material from a range of authors on the relationships between science, religion, and theology. Topics include: models of interaction between science and religion, historical reflections on the 'conflict thesis', scientific and theological methods, creation and modern cosmology, uncertainty and chaos, creationism and evolutionary theory, the anthropic principle and design, and the challenge of reductionism.

British Humanist Association: www.humanism.org.uk/education

From this web link you can find pages for teachers and students to support education about humanism.

Counterbalance: www.counterbalance.org/

This American-based organization, the Counterbalance Interactive Library, has articles and opinion pieces on a range of science, ethics, philosophy and religion topics.

Ephron, N. J. (2006) *Judaism and Science: A Historical Introduction*. London: Greenwood Press.

This book looks at Jewish attitudes towards nature and its study. It explores questions about the complex relationship between religion and science, including: How did religious attitudes and doctrines affect Jewish attitudes towards natural knowledge? How was Jewish interest in science reflected, and facilitated by, links with other cultures? The book also considers the attitudes and work of particular Jews in different epochs.

Iqbal, M. (2002) *Islam and Science*. Aldershot: Ashgate.

This book aims to provide an understanding of the contemporary relationship between Islam and modern science by exploring the historical and cultural forces that have shaped and defined Muslim attitudes towards science.

National Secular Society (NSS): www.secularism.org.uk/resources. html

The NSS campaigns 'against the undue influence of religion in public affairs and education'. The web links to articles supporting and promoting scientific rationalism.

O'Leary, D. (2006) *Roman Catholicism and Modern Science: A History*. London: Continuum.

This book is an historical treatment of Catholic attitudes toward science after Galileo. The book examines Catholicism's changing responses to Darwinian evolution, and contemporary debates surrounding agnosticism, biblical criticism, the philosophy and professionalization of science, contraception, 'in vitro' fertilization, gene therapy, experimentation on embryos and organ transplantation.

Peters, T. Iqbal, M. and Nomanul Haq, S. (eds) (2002) *God, Life and the Cosmos*. Aldershot: Ashgate.

In this book, Christian and Muslim scholars explore key issues in science and religion from Christian and Islamic perspectives, examining the philosophical issues in science-religion discourse, cosmology and bioethics.

Poole, M. W. (2007) *User's Guide to Science and Belief*. Oxford: Lion Hudson.

This book explores the interaction between science and religious belief for both the general reader and students. Subjects covered include: Do science and the Bible contradict each other? Is faith believing what you know isn't true? Has the work of Darwin ruled out the idea of a creating God?

Richardson, W. M. and Wildman, W. J. (eds) (1996) *Religion and Science: History, Method, Dialogue*. London: Routledge.

This book emphasises the historical, methodological, and constructive dimensions in the religion and science debate. It examines the interaction between science and religion in several periods since the European Enlightenment; the similarities and differences between the methods of science and religious studies and also includes case studies exemplifying the dialogue between important theories in the natural sciences and key religious topics.

Science & Spirit magazine:

Based in Washington, USA, this web magazine aims to explore 'the intersection of science, religion, and culture', showing 'how technology, faith, ethics, and the arts connect in both global affairs and our everyday lives'.

Southgate, C. (ed.) (2005) *God, Humanity and the Cosmos*. London: T & T Clark.

This book explores contemporary perspectives in physics, evolutionary biology and psychology as they relate to theological descriptions of the universe, humanity and consciousness, and surveys the theological, philosophical and historical issues underpinning the science-religion debate.

UCCF: The Christian Unions: www.bethinking.org

This website provides a range of articles on apologetics – including science – to 'help you to understand, defend and communicate the Christian faith'.

Here are some sources that focus on our understanding of biology and human origins:

Richard Dawkins website: http://richarddawkins.net/

A comprehensive website focusing on Dawkins' books, articles and opinion pieces, plus links to the numerous electronic fora discussing related issues.

Fuller, S. (2007) *Science vs. Religion: Intelligent Design and the Problem of Evolution*. Cambridge: Polity Press.

This book focuses on the debates about evolution and intelligent design theory, and the struggle between State and Church as sources of legitimate authority.

Messer, N. (2007) *Selfish Genes and Christian Ethics: The Theological-Ethical Implications of Evolutionary Biology*. London: SCM.

This book aims to provide a Christian theological anthropology, to 'give Christians and the churches the confidence to engage with assumptions that evolutionary theory and religious beliefs are untenable' and 'the practical questions raised by evolutionary discussions of ethics and morality'.

Ruse, M. (2005) *The Evolution–Creation Struggle*. London: Harvard University Press.

This book is an historical account of the roots of today's creation versus evolution controversy as responses to a loss of religious faith in the Western world.

Here are some books that principally focus on physics and cosmological issues:

Barrow, J. D. and Tipler, F. J. (1988) *The Anthropic Cosmological Principle*. Oxford: Oxford University Press.

This book examines the question of mankind's place in the universe, and issues such as the nature of life, the search for extraterrestrial intelligence, and the past history and fate of our universe.

Close, F. (2006) *The New Cosmic Onion*. Oxford: Taylor & Francis.

The book's original title was used as a metaphor for the layers that can be peeled away to understand the foundations of the physical world, from dimensions and galaxies, to atoms and quarks. This updated version looks at contemporary scientific accounts of the universe, and the forces of nature to be found in atoms, the nucleus and nuclear particles.

Davies, P. (2006) *God & the New Physics*. Harmondsworth: Penguin.

This book aims to give an explanation of how recent discoveries of the new physics are changing 'our view of the world and, in particular, throwing light on many of the questions formerly posed by religion'.

Holder, R. D. (2004) *God, the Multiverse and Everything*. Aldershot: Ashgate.

This book argues that 'divine design is the best explanation for cosmic fine-tuning', and that 'design by God is a superior explanation in terms of both initial plausibility and explanatory power, and is therefore the most rational position to take on the basis of the cosmological data'.

Weinberg, S. (1993) *The First Three Minutes: A Modern View of the Origin of the Universe*. New York: Basic Books.

A classic, contemporary physics account for the general reader, as to what happened when the universe began, and how we know.

Part I

Developing a pedagogical framework

Chapter 2

Why teach religion and science?

Chapter overview

This chapter looks at two particular ways of thinking, or habits of mind: the religious and the scientific. The way we make sense of things has a direct impact on our teaching and learning, and in this chapter we discuss why viewing the world through a scientific lens might also help you and your students' religious education.

The spiritual side to science

It can be argued that a spiritual sense is a prerequisite for learning. It is a way to reach *beyond* our selves and our existing knowledge and is the impetus to our search for explanations. This does *not* necessarily imply a religious quest, although it is strongly argued by many that a spiritual education is only educationally meaningful when taught as part of a religious tradition. However, even the writings of some of the most strident of scientific materialists, such as Carl Sagan or Daniel Dennett, acknowledge that the learning and understanding that comes from a scientific *engagement* with the world requires a similarly spiritual view of science. Here, it is the science and not the individual or scientist that is important. Hence, a growing awareness of the power we have to shape our surroundings and what can be gained from our developing knowledge and understanding of scientific information about ourselves, and our environment, *should* be enough to humble any individual. Therefore, an increasing unfolding of the subtleties, complexities and beauty of the natural world *would* allow one to gain a more 'realistic' perspective of human ideas, actions and beliefs, and their 'place' in the physical world – our spiritual development comes from our exploration and deepening appreciation of Nature's workings. To those of you who understand 'spiritual' in a religious sense, this may seem incongruous. Yet the growing importance of students to be 'educated' and 'informed' about concepts such as 'human impact' on the environment, and the introduction of related topics into the religious education curriculum, both imply that the values and philosophies consciously and unconsciously conveyed by contemporary scientific thinking need full and careful consideration by your students.

Pause for reflection

What is your reaction to our suggestion that science also has a spiritual dimension? Does spiritual experience always have to be linked to religious faith?

Do any of the following comments chime with your own view? What is your reaction to the range of views expressed?

I believe in a higher authority, an external power – whether that is God or Allah. We develop by becoming involved with and participating in that belief. You have to allow that to take up the forefront of your mind rather than focusing on the mundane.

I would describe myself as someone who is spiritual. It is about contemplation and your feelings about various things in life. I don't think that being spiritual means that you are by definition religious. I think that although I am spiritual and I have beliefs and ideas about faith, I am not a member of a religious organization. I don't have a religion, but if you are religious this has to be interlinked with spirituality.

I just connect spirituality with religion; to me your spiritual self is your religion – your appreciation of something else apart from the actual world. So if you're not religious, or you don't think there is anything else out there, you're not spiritual.

It is about someone's sense of what's going on around them and outside of their immediate environment. It is about the feelings and emotions – not just religion and beliefs – and interpreting things as something more than the literal.

I see myself as part of a bigger cycle of things: in terms of humanity, but also in terms of the planet and your own place on that planet.

Comment

For science's ideas and explanations to have any relevance to the way you and your students learn and teach religious education, your recognition of science as one of the ways of understanding our relationship to others is required; science increases substantiates and authenticates our relationships with people, nature and the natural world. Connecting science to the individual (student and teacher), through its implications for the study of other disciplines (such as religious education), transforms it into an intermediary for social cohesion, by which your students can find and establish a stronger relationship to people, nature and society – instead of feeling disconnected and distanced from others. For you to do this, you must be able to articulate a view of science that is not only personally meaningful but also accurately reflective of the spirit of its endeavour.

Our aim is to show you a way of supporting your students as they explore their developing understanding of their relationships to other people and their environment, and to do this in a way that allows *all* your students to participate.

Pause for reflection

How well does your present approach to teaching religious education allow individuals with no professed religious faith to develop spiritually? How would you respond, if your students said the following?

One of my friends is a strong Christian but, as I'm strongly against organized religions, I don't believe that we should be told what to do. You should do what you want to do if you think it's morally right.

I'm interested in what people get from their religion, it then gives me extra ideas, and sometimes makes me feel like: 'I wish I had something like that in my life' but I don't, because I'm not religious.

I'm not religious but I have many Muslim, Sikh and Catholic friends who have similar outlooks on the world. It makes you think more about things and makes me think what I agree with and what of my friends' beliefs I reject and why. In a way I'd be most comfortable with a religion that takes the best bits from them all!

My experiences of people around me, friends that follow a religious faith, provoke me to wonder about things – not just positive things but also those that cause sadness – and see why they think the way they do.

Comment

What we hope to encourage is an approach to the teaching of religious education that will allow your students to speak about the spiritual in terms that go beyond the individual self to find engagement with something that is 'universal' and pan-human, and allow your students' scientific and spiritual educations to go hand–in–hand as they accrue knowledge and skills to make sense of the world. Indeed, the development of personal explanations while respecting alternate views when exploring controversial socio–scientific issues is exactly just such an example of this happening in practice. This would allow your students to develop their self–worth and self–esteem as they become able to objectively criticize their own work and make honest, but fair responses to critical observations or arguments made by their peers. Students may also be called upon to promote or find value in another's ideas, which may differ markedly from their own, or be called upon to undertake creative or imaginative investigations of questions raised by these 'alternative' ideas.

Meaningful science

As well as supplying factual information, scientific knowledge brings with it an appreciation of the need for individual humility and awareness that the achievements of science and technology – for example, the Apollo Moon landings, or the development of the MRI body scanner – are the results of a shared, collective endeavour. The teaching of religion and science topics is an opportunity to examine an important aspect of our humanity and, in doing so, your students will have the opportunity to develop a sense of fellowship with other human beings, and view the different ways human beings have explored, examined, understood and made meanings about the physical world.

An understanding of the practices of science and scientists will also require your students to appreciate that to *do* science also necessitates a drive to find things out, to seek a collective understanding of ourselves and the world we inhabit, *and that it is within all of us*. What is clear is that your students need to be given the opportunity to explore and develop a voice to express *what science means to them*. This may be achieved through fostering the transformative, aesthetic experiences of your students, and one of the most effective ways of doing this is by engaging their sense of wonder.

Why learn about religion *and* science?

Scientists and philosophers of science have long appreciated the value of having a developed sense of wonder when trying to understand physical processes. Indeed, for many scientists, wonder is inseparable from the study of Nature and its processes, and is maintained and needs to be nourished in the young by adults. It is not, therefore, a passive experiencing of the natural world, but an active engagement with and discovery of its underlying processes.

One of the most effective ways of achieving this when teaching religion and science is for you to appreciate the value of an emotional engagement with scientific information underpinning the issues you will teach. To do this you will need to recognize, acknowledge and then accommodate these opportunities within your teaching. The ability to give ourselves over to wonder – reflecting on science's possible meanings, rather than merely commenting on the science described – will also facilitate your students' critical thinking, and enhance their capacities, in reasoning and their ability to perceive connections, consequences, inconsistencies and flaws, that, we hope, are being developed by our teaching:

> The trip to the mountain top was very beautiful. We saw glacial pools. I always remember looking down, and, wow, realising that we've walked all the way up! Look how beautiful everything is – crystal clear water, wow! Knowing all the processes that went on, the geological terms for everything and trying to imagine the glaciers when they were there, what they did and how it all worked and how long it took! The won-derment of all of that, that nature can do that to a landscape and make it so beautiful.

> I remember, by accident, catching a partial lunar eclipse. I can remem-ber looking outside and seeing that the Moon had gone a very strange colour and just standing and standing there. The realisation of what was happening, and particularly the personal discovery, brings with it the wonderment.

The paradoxical nature of wonder

Most aesthetic experiences also produce a physical reaction. It is not just the memory of a beautiful scene, but the response to the event that becomes memorable and meaningful:

Going up in the plane I could see all the science behind the clouds and how they're formed and looking down at the ground and thinking . . . How has the Earth been formed and created and how is it sustaining itself?

Another important aspect of our intellectual engagement with wonder is our need to accommodate such events within our own narratives and make them personally important. It is only then that the individual moves from the passive viewer of beauty to being an active thinker. The event becomes meaningful and requires an explanation:

When I was younger I was quite scared about the origins of the Universe, that there was this big void out there, and it was more of a comfort to think that it was created by God . . . I've now got a more of a scientific view on things, and it is amazing that it has created – out of itself – something as fantastic as that!

Here is the Socratic notion of philosophy beginning in wonder – knowing one's ignorance, knowing what one does not know – is driving and sustaining the individual's need to seek intelligibility.

This would, however, appear to raise an obvious paradox namely, that there is decay in our appreciation of wonder as we get older, which appears to be matched by our increasing knowledge and understanding of the very events being observed. Wonder is most likely to appear to the young student when experiences are limited or little thought has been given over to a particular issue:

I first saw thunder and lightning when I was little, and it seemed amazing what was going on – when you're little, you create little stories about what is happening. Later on, when you're older and you find out about it this lessens the wonder because you're not wondering anymore, you know that's why it does that, whereas before you don't know and that makes it more fascinating.

It is, however, only with experience that we are able to *recognize* the significance of an event and its *relationship* to the others things we know:

> You can read and hear about them, but you only appreciate them when you see it take place – particularly a solar eclipse or the Boxing Day tsunami. The vastness as you understand the scale and the proportions of what has happened is just amazing!

Through wonder to the transcendent

Unfortunately, for many of your students, scientific reasoning is at best unnecessary or, at worst, an intrusion. Science is somehow perceived as being at odds with what is of personal importance; it explains everything, apart from what we want to really know about – ourselves. Its perceived purity, logic and amorality denude it of those very human characteristics that helps us to give meaning to our lives and actions.

Many rationalists would wish this divide be maintained and even emphasized, as it is the 'delusions' of religio-cultural societies that stop human beings from developing a more realistic meaning for their lives. What is not, however, disputed, is that the experiential realities that shape our everyday lives are important *to us*, *need* to be explained and should not be ignored.

So when the wonder evoked (by the birth of a child or looking at the stars) is used by us to explore questions that have a wider consequence, we have moved beyond an emotional response to an external stimulus, to the realisation that the event lived through could be life changing. If the wonder is imbued with an enduring meaning for the individual it may, consequently, have the power to transcend the event to transform the very way they understand themselves and the world they inhabit.

Here is one way you can help your students to appreciate the similarities and differences between the way science and religions are involved to make sense of our experiences: allow your students to reflect on experiences that evoke transformative wonder; wonder that has an enduring effect and is personally meaningful can transform the way one makes sense of the world.

Further reading

Dennett, D. C. (2006) *Breaking the Spell: Religion as a Natural Phenomenon.* New York: Allen Lane.

'Few forces in the world are as potent as religion: it comforts people in their suffering and inspires them to both magnificent and terrible deeds.' This book 'seeks to uncover the origins of religion and discusses how and why different faiths have shaped so many lives, whether religion is an addiction or a genuine human need, and even whether it is good for our health'.

Fisher, P. (1998) *Wonder, the Rainbow and the Aesthetics of Rare Experiences.* Cambridge, MA: Harvard University Press.

This book is about wonder in relation to the visual world, and how we should view the relationship between aesthetic and scientific understandings of the world.

Midgley, M. (1992) *Science as Salvation: A Modern Myth and its Meaning.* London: Routledge.

This book argues that 'science has developed high spiritual ambitions', and that 'from prophetic physicists have come speculations that go beyond the claims of any religion'.

Polkinghorne, J. (1996) *Beyond Science.* Cambridge: Cambridge University Press.

This book 'goes beyond science to consider the human context in which it operates and to pursue that wider understanding which we all seek', as well as its place in human culture.

Trigg, R. (1998) *Rationality and Religion: Does Faith Need Reason?.* Oxford: Blackwell.

This book tries to answer the question of how far religious faith needs reason.

Chapter 3

Understanding different attitudes to religion and science

Chapter overview

This chapter aims to enable you to reflect on and become aware of the individual differences in the way people view and perceive scientific knowledge, and how this might affect the way we understand its relationship to religious issues. The chapter then goes on to address the implications this has for the way we should approach our teaching of religion and science issues and, if also applicable to your students, reflects on how such differences may influence the way religion and science topics are learnt.

Attitudes to science

What we believe, and the knowledge we act upon, is guided by ways of thinking that mostly go unnoticed or, at the very least, are only reflected on occasionally – perhaps at times of personal crisis. However, one of the many roles a teacher has to perform in his/her class is to facilitate students to undertake this task explicitly as part of their everyday schooling. The experienced professional would also be expected to reflect upon their own beliefs and values and how they shape their teaching practice as part of their continuing professional development.

RE teachers are not known to be 'scientifically minded' and are more likely to have science backgrounds similar to the lay public than their science teacher colleagues. Some may even possess belief systems that are alienated from the scientific orthodoxy, so for you to be able to understand your students' beliefs and approaches to science *you* must also look at what contributes to your own ideas about science. This will allow you to develop practices that might then enable you to reflect on what actually informs your own approach, rather than be told in this book what you should believe – a strategy that is unlikely to be successful!

Ways of viewing religion and science

Helping you to develop such an understanding should help to give you a way of appreciating how people relate religion and science.

Point for reflection

As an initial gauge of your 'attitude' to the role, purpose and impact of science, how would you respond to the following statements?

- Science will help to make the world a better place in the future.
- Scientific discoveries do more harm than good.
- Scientific inventions improve our standard of living.
- Much of the anxiety in modern society is due to science.
- Money spent on science is well worth spending.
- Science and technology are the cause of many of the world's problems.
- Science is useful for solving the problems of everyday life.
- Scientific inventions have increased tensions between people.

Are your responses consistent? If you find some statements difficult to answer or you are ambivalent, reflect on why this might be the case.

Comment

We would hope that you would share our belief that a good religious education teacher – like all teachers – should foster in their students an openness to argument and evidence, and scepticism and objectivity are to be encouraged. As we have argued in Chapter 2, we feel that exploring religion and science topics will benefit your attempts to develop these qualities in your students. This might not, however, be shared by everyone. Any resistance or ambivalence to this suggestion should be linked to understanding what might lie behind observed attitudes to science. Personal views are necessarily complex and may lack internal consistency, with views stubbornly refusing to fit into a clearly defined category.

Point for reflection

What are your responses to the following questions? Do you think your religious education colleagues would agree with you? What about your fellow professionals in the Science Department?

- What, in your opinion, is the relevance of teaching religion and science topics?
- Should your views on science influence how religious education should be taught?
- Should science influence the practice and content of RE?
- Should the religious beliefs – or lack of them – of your students affect the way you teach RE?

Comment: are religion and science essential to your way of thinking?

We hope that the above 'point for reflection' has helped you to appreciate that the way you view and use scientific knowledge might not necessarily be shared by your colleagues and, most importantly, by your students.

Individuals appear to hold a range of views about science and religion and their relative importance in making sense of the world and the decisions they make. For some, one or both are integral in shaping the individual's whole thinking, not just when considering unambiguously scientific or religious issues but also essential to the way they make sense of their morals and values. For others, religion and/or science maybe viewed best as 'tools' that people have developed and contain knowledge and skills that need to be learnt to help them resolve problems and improve their lot. Any utility beyond their particular domain is perceived to be limited or of little relevance when trying to answer more fundamental concerns.

Activity

What is your response to the following statements about studying religion and science? Which student would you find most difficult to accommodate into your teaching and why?

I tend to use both ways of thinking to find my way around – trying to work out answers to the questions of life. Everyone has a hunger to know basic questions, such as: Why are we here? You answer them at different levels, but they are interlinked.

Science is a religion and that you're accepting it's based largely on faith – faith in Einstein and Newton.

In general, the religion and science are very close. The scientists will try to answer the questions why and will go deeper and deeper. They get to the stage when, if they are a religious person, then their religion will take over, but it's not a big difference.

What's the point of studying this sort of stuff? We're never going to find a 100 per cent answer. You can never come up with 100 per cent evidence, and even some of the strongest Christians will have doubts and some of the best scientists get it wrong. They can say, factually, 'That's definitely true' and then a hundred years later we find they were wrong.

Scientific thinking goes on the basis of how you think something works. Religious thinking is from within the heart and applies to everyday life.

You can't run your life using science. The decisions you make are as much about how you feel – and this is closer to religious thinking, which is about morality and our attitude to other people.

There are certain boundaries where science can't cross, where science has to stop and religion or Christianity, or the Bible, carries on.

It seems that science ought to tell you 'yes' or 'no' and it doesn't, which is just frustrating, but it makes it fun to think about. I think there is a certainty and, yes, science ought to discover that certainty.

I think that science is quite like a religion anyway, as nothing is definite. Science is still a belief in what you have done.

Everybody should be curious about the world around them. Science can also help tackle the deeper side of things; it's more about you, more personal, you don't have to read a book to get an answer, it's more about looking inside you.

I personally believe that God created the world and that science is part of that world. I think that it can't just be chance and evolution. There must be something more going on than just chance.

One of my problems with religion is that lots of religions kind of indoctrinate you from a very early age – it's difficult to change views as you get older. I don't really agree with that, I think people should have a broad awareness of all the different aspects of things and then come to their own conclusions.

Implications for teaching and learning

There are obviously differences in the extent to which students will make use of scientific knowledge in developing their personal views and opinions. For you, their teacher, this has implications for the effectiveness of your teaching. Some of your students may already have a strongly developed sense of the context for their own beliefs and attitudes in relation to science and religion. Some students may come to your class with exactly the opposite attitudes! For others, differences may be much more subtle and their resulting responses to a particular religion and science topic will be much more nuanced.

Some students will view scientific knowledge – especially when supported by concrete evidence and facts – as an importance source when developing their ideas about the world, whereas others would not consider using scientific evidence to change their own, never mind other people's, opinions. So what might be an effective way of teaching religion and science? Are teachers ready to accept that some of their students will believe that there is a *de facto* connection between scientific ways of making sense of the world and the content of religious education, whilst others will hold the diametrically opposed belief? Is there an approach that could accommodate such a diversity of views?

We appreciate that it would be easy for you to ignore or dismiss these questions as an irrelevance to the main goals of religious education. We have already tried, in the previous chapter, to explain why we think it is to your advantage to explore religion and science topics. Indeed, you may already be convinced of the desirability of teaching such topics but are deterred by the difficulties we've highlighted. Addressing this concern is the aim of the remainder of this book. Our pedagogical approach is explained in the next chapter, and how this might be put into practice in Part 2.

Further reading

Barbour, I. G. (1998) *Religion and Science: Historical and Contemporary Issues*. London: SCM.

This is one of the main contemporary texts discussing the many issues surrounding God, religious 'truths' and experiences in a 'scientific age'.

Drees, W. B. (1996) *Religion, Science and Naturalism*. Cambridge: Cambridge University Press.
This book considers the consequences of the natural sciences for our view of the world. The book also argues that both religion and morality should be viewed as natural phenomena; they have their development in our evolutionary past and our 'neurophysiological constitution'.

Peacock, A. (1993) *Theology for a Scientific Age*. London: SCM.
The aim of this book is to 'present a theology that is plausible, believable, defensible – and therefore relevant – to those who take seriously established scientific knowledge of the world and who seek meaning in a world so described'.

Polkinghorne, H. (1996) *Scientists as Theologians*. London: SPCK.
This book surveys and outlines the similarities and differences in the ideas of three notable scientist-theologians: Ian Barbour, Arthur Peacocke and John Polkinghorne.

Rupke, N. A. (2009) *Eminent Lives in Twentieth-Century Science and Religion*, 2nd edn. New York: Peter Laing.
Eminent scientists' – such as Carson, Pavlov, Einstein, and Wilson – views on religion and its relevance and relationship to their scientific work and understanding are examined.

Chapter 4

Developing a pedagogical approach

Chapter overview

In this chapter we are interested in how you position yourself with regard to religious education pedagogy. There can be many reasons for the way in which teachers understand pedagogy and their preferences for one pedagogical approach over another. However, one thing that can be said straightaway is that religious education has traditionally been a much-contested subject with regard to approaches to teaching and learning. To begin with, religious education means different things to different people. For example, as we mentioned in Chapter 1, the UK is fairly unique in that within state schools 'religious education' does not mean a faith-based nurturing approach to teaching religion. Understandably then, because of this, how the teaching of religion is, and has been, understood in schools in England has often courted controversy.

In this chapter, we look at how religious education teaching strategies can best grow and emerge from an understanding of the pedagogical approach within which you are working. We then describe how a pedagogy, based on a clear appreciation of what is actually meant by phenomenological religious education, will give you an effective way of engaging with religion and science issues within a religious education curriculum.

What are the aims and purposes of RE?

Activity

Look at the selection of quotations below from religious education literature that were comments on the first truly multi-faith religious education syllabus developed in Birmingham in the 1970s. Do they remind you of any contemporary concerns regarding the aims and purposes of RE? How has the current debate 'moved on', if at all, from the one that took place in the 1970s?

> One has to ask, what is its *operative* rationale? Does it look on religious education as the acquiring of blocks of knowledge about life stances, only some of which can be considered because there are so many of them? Or does it regard the subject as enabling pupils to shop around among those religions and life stances that appeal to them in order to 'find a faith to live by? . . . Or does it indeed envisage religious education as giving skills to understand basic human beliefs and motivations and conveying the ability to be consciously discriminating in a pluralistic age? . . . Or are all these three views operative in different parts?'
> [Cox, E. (1976) 'Does it do as it says?' *Learning for Living*, 15(4): 125–126.]

> Generalisations are attempted which are far in advance of evidence; it has been impossible to operationally achieve its aims. Thus it is that religious education has attempted too much and achieved too little.
> [Lupton, H. E. (1975) 'Checklist for Study of the Religious Education Syllabus' *Learning for Living*, 14(4): 134–137.]

Continuing controversy, such as the legal wrangle over Birmingham's new syllabus, gives emphasis to the fact that one *still* cannot find an unequivocal answer to the question, what are the purposes and contents proper to religious education in county schools?

[Webster, D. (1976) 'Theory in Religious Education: Criticism and Prospect' *Learning for Living*, 15(3): 85–90.]

Comment

In 1994 the Schools Curriculum and Assessment Authority (SCAA) published two 'model syllabuses' for religious education, which included what they believed to be the aims of the subject. In effect SCAA restated what had come to be regarded as the aims of the subject published in a succession of agreed syllabuses during the previous decade or so. What must be remembered, however, is that this is not the same as stating the purpose of religious education. SCAA's three main aims were:

1 To enable pupils to gain knowledge and understanding of religion(s).
2 To promote understanding of and respect for people whose cultures and beliefs are different from one's own, and to promote a positive attitude towards living in a plural society.
3 To promote the personal, moral and spiritual development of pupils.

These could be regarded as complementary aims for the subject but in effect they represent different answers to the question, 'what is the purpose of RE?' Each reflects a particular view of the purpose of religious education, which are not necessarily complementary, and each makes different demands on teachers.

Activity

How have RE syllabuses, curricula documents and reviews prioritized these aims in your view? Do we need to prioritize these aims? If so, how?

Comment

One way of looking at this is to compare how religious education and science are understood in the National Curriculum. From September 2007, religious education became a National Curriculum subject in English and Welsh secondary schools, albeit as a non-statutory one. The new 'National Curriculum' in religious education is based on the October 2004 *Non-statutory National Framework for Religious Education*. This is helpful for our purposes because in this introductory section we are able to compare certain aspects of the National Curriculum in science and religious education and draw some conclusions that can help us in developing appropriate pedagogy.

The importance of science and RE

Activity

Examine the two 'importance of' statements for science and religious education and consider how they differ, and what elements they have in common? Why do you think the first statement focuses on science and not on science education? Is there anything missing from the statement about religious education?

The importance of science:

The study of science fires pupils' curiosity about phenomena in the world around them and offers opportunities to find explanations. It engages learners at many levels, linking direct practical experience with scientific ideas. Experimentation and modelling are used to develop and evaluate explanations, encouraging critical and creative thought. Pupils learn how knowledge and understanding in science are rooted in evidence. They discover how scientific ideas contribute to technological change – affecting industry, business and medicine, and improving quality of life. They trace the development of science worldwide and recognize its cultural significance. They learn to question and discuss issues that may affect their own lives, and directions of societies and the future of the world.

The importance of religious education:

Religious education provokes challenging questions about the ultimate meaning and purpose of life, beliefs about God, the self and the nature of reality, issues of right and wrong, and what it means to be human. It develops pupils' knowledge and understanding of Christianity, other principal religions, other religious traditions, and other world views that offer answers to these challenging questions. It offers opportunities for personal reflection and spiritual development. It enhances pupils' awareness and understanding of religious beliefs, teachings, practices and forms of expression, as well as of the influence of religion on individuals, families, communities and cultures.

Religious education encourages pupils to learn from different religions, beliefs, values and traditions while exploring their own beliefs and questions of meaning. It challenges pupils to reflect on, consider, analyse, interpret and evaluate issues of truth, belief, faith and ethics and to communicate their responses.

> Religious education encourages pupils to develop their sense of identity and belonging. It enables them to flourish individually within their communities and as citizens in a diverse society and global community. Religious education has an important role in preparing pupils for adult life, employment and lifelong learning. It enables them to develop respect and sensitivity for others, in particular those with faiths and beliefs different from their own. It promotes discernment and enables pupils to combat prejudice.

Comment

The science statement makes a case for the distinctiveness of science as an academic discipline that views the world from a particular perspective and employs certain types of methodology in its study, with the emphasis being on the study of phenomena and their explanation based on evidence.

The religious education statement attempts to make a case for the distinctiveness of the study of religion but, in our opinion, with less success. It begins: 'Religious Education provokes challenging questions about the ultimate meaning and purpose of life, beliefs about God, the self and the nature of reality, issues of right and wrong and what it means to be human'. As a statement about the process of religious education, this is an accurate statement of recent good practice in the subject. But, does it define what is distinctive about religious education? Some might answer in the affirmative asking where else in the curriculum is there a place for pupils to engage with these questions and issues? And this is a fair question. But is this *necessarily* the case? Do students have to study *religious* education to study beliefs about God? Cannot and do not sociologists, historians and anthropologists study such matters? Does not literature offer ample opportunities to study what it means to be human? One could ask similar questions about the other claims for religious education contained in this statement.

Transcendent RE

One of the things that distinguish a religious view of the world from a materialist view is the belief in God or, more helpfully, the transcendent.

We would suggest that what is missing from the 'importance of' statement for religious education is that, whilst religion does provoke and answer questions about what it means to be human arising out of and relating to different spiritual and cultural traditions, all religions are concerned with human transformation, and religion enables its adherents to understand the world in terms of a *transcendent dimension* to life. We develop this further later in the chapter.

As we have tried to show in Chapter 3, and again in Chapter 6, people have quite different views about how they understand religion and science. Often science is seen as based on evidence about the world, while religion is seen as involving beliefs based on faith and is, therefore, necessarily more controversial than science.

Such a view is largely responsible for the adoption of a phenomenological approach to the study of religion, which treats religion as a phenomenon that can be studied objectively much like one might study other phenomena in the world. Because of this, modern religious education has recently been characterized as overly descriptive of religious beliefs and practices and not concerned enough with their truth and philosophical claims. While this should not necessarily have been the case in a subject deriving its *modus operandi* from the work of Ninian Smart, it is easy to understand how the subject, in some cases, has become a branch of citizenship or social studies concerned with the accurate description of religions with a view to creating social cohesion and tolerance. And, as we noted above, the perceived confusion of aims for religious education does not help.

One thing that does need pointing out, however, is that there is a difference between having aims for a subject and clearly articulating what the subject's purpose is – both need to be understood.

Our preferred answer to the prioritizing of aims is to say that religious education is at its best when it is concerned with interpreting religion in relation to human experience and supporting students in developing their own values and principles. So, on this basis:

- The purpose of religious education is to promote the personal, moral and spiritual development of pupils (*main aim*).
- The purpose of religious education is to enable pupils to gain knowledge and understanding of religion(s) (*instrumental aim*).
- The purpose of religious education is to promote understanding of, and respect for, people whose cultures and beliefs are different from one's own and to promote a positive attitude towards living in a plural society (*consequential aim*).

We will unpack what we mean by this in what follows: initially in this chapter and then in subsequent chapters and the example lessons in Chapters 7 and 8.

The epistemological issue

One objection to what has been said above is that epistemologically speaking we know that science deals with the physical world: in empirical evidence, hypotheses and develops theories arising out of these, whereas religion's main subject matter is not physical and lacks empirical evidence. Consequently, it is easy to see the value of science to a students' education but less so religion. So maybe a kind of sociological emphasis is the best way forward for religious education? As John Hick has pointed out, 'Naturalism has created the "consensus reality" of our culture. It has become so ingrained that we no longer see it, but see everything else through it' (Hick 1999: 14).

But, as Hick also points out, as far as we can understand the universe, we find it to be ambiguous. As conceived by us, the universe can have a naturalistic or religious character and it is not the case that a naturalistic interpretation is rational and a religious interpretation is irrational. For whilst it is perfectly possible to interpret and describe the universe in purely naturalistic terms, it is also equally possible to describe it, 'in ways that accept most of the naturalistic account but set this in the context of a more encompassing spirituality' (Hick 1999: 15).

We have already seen how individuals might think about religion and science in Chapter 3 and we have given some examples of how it is possible for a person to accommodate both modes of meaning in their thinking.

Pedagogy

So what does all this mean for our attempt to develop effective pedagogies for teaching about religion and science? Let's begin by looking at some recent criticisms of religious education pedagogy.

The 2007 Ofsted report, *Making Sense of Religion* made the following critical remarks:

> In many cases, teachers perceive that AT1 work is essentially descriptive and a lower order of challenge. They assume that short answers are all that is required to check basic knowledge and understanding. More extended answers are always linked to AT2 alone. As a result, AT1 tasks too often demand that pupils 'report on' or 'write about' rather than asking them to analyse and process the material.
>
> [Ofsted 2007: 10]

> Unevenness in the progress that pupils make across the two attainment targets of 'learning about' and 'learning from' religion reflects the continuing emphasis that many schools place on 'learning about' religion. Where provision is particularly weak, pupils learn about only superficial features of the religion, rather than deepening their understanding through investigation. This tends to happen when teachers assume that more analytical and reflective tasks are linked predominantly to attainment target 2, 'learning from' religion; as a result, they do not include challenging tasks in work related to 'learning about' religion.
>
> [Ofsted 2007: 38]

Such comments from Ofsted echo this trenchant criticism made by Michael Grimmitt:

> Where teachers attempt to encourage pupils to learn from religions it falls short of the pedagogical strategy which the original concept involved, namely that pupils should evaluate their understanding of religion in personal terms and evaluate their understanding of self in religious terms. In other words, the evaluative process of learning from

religion(s) should be fully integrated into how, within a secular educational context, pupils are learning about religions in the first place.

[Grimmitt 2000: 15]

Religion and meaning

We have explored in Chapter 2 the notion of 'meaningful science'. Can
we talk about religion in the same kind of way? What might we mean by
'meaningful religion' in terms of religious education pedagogy?

Considering the criticisms noted above, it would seem that the key to
a good pedagogy is an appropriate understanding of how pupils are to
learn about the subject. In the case of religious education, the question is
not just 'how are they to study religion?' but 'what are they to study when
studying religion?'

Traditionally there have been two ways of understanding religious
faith. The first one might be referred to as propositional and the second
experiential.

Propositional faith is probably the more common understanding of
religion as assent to divinely revealed propositions. This is what religious
people 'believe'. It is an interpretation of religion most commonly attacked
by 'new atheists' such as Richard Dawkins. The alternative experiential
understanding, is when a religious faith consists of a free interpretation of
the religious person's experience of the world, lived in the presence of the
divine or the transcendent.

The American historian of religion Wilfred Cantwell Smith expressed
this well in his 1963 book entitled *The Meaning and End of Religion*, when
he wrote:

> Those of us on the outside who would interpret to ourselves the
> Muslim must understand not his religion but his religiousness.
>
> So for the Hindu, the Buddhist, the Tierra del Fuegin. If we would
> comprehend these we must look not at their religion but at the universe
> so far as possible through their eyes. It is what the Hindu is able to see,
> by being a Hindu that is significant. Until we can see it too, we have
> not come to grips with the religious quality of his life. And we can be

sure that when he looks around him he does not see 'Hinduism'. Like the rest of us, he sees his wife's death, his child's minor and major aspirations, his money lender's mercilessness, the calm of a starlight evening, his own mortality. He sees things through coloured glasses, if one will, of a 'Hindu' brand.

Pedagogies of religious education

Ever since religious education in the UK rejected a narrow biblically based Christian education, it has struggled to articulate an approach to the teaching and learning of religion that meets universal approval. Ninian Smart's phenomenological approach to religious education was influenced not only by continental phenomenology but also by twentieth-century liberal Christian theology. Such influences resulted in a number of distinct criticisms of Smart's approach and its contemporary manifestations, all of which, to some degree, emanate from a misinterpretation of Smart's early writings.

Criticisms of phenomenological religious education

In recent years there have been criticisms of the phenomenological approach. We have looked at some of these criticisms such as the comments from Ofsted outlined above. A major criticism is that phenomenological religious education has failed to engage students' critical faculties, being no more than a descriptive labelling of religious beliefs and practices.

It is, however, doubtful that Smart's early work on a phenomenological approach can be found guilty of this. In his famous book *Secular Education and the Logic of Religion*, Smart distinguishes between the *historical* and the *parahistorical*. 'We can consider religious phenomena and beliefs from a purely historical and descriptive point of view on the one hand; and we can approach them as relevant to, or as enshrining, claims about the nature of reality' (1968: 12). He refers to the former as historical and the latter as parahistorical. He prefers the term parahistorical to 'doctrinal' because the doctrinal only represents one dimension of religion. The parahistorical refers to:

... cases of commending the faith, of arguing for its truth, of endorsing religious values etc., and cases of doing the reverse (as when one may criticise the faith as untrue, or dangerous, or decadent, or pernicious, or nonsensical etc.).

[Smart 1968: 13]

Therefore a study of religion that only concentrates on one of these is unbalanced. To emphasize only the descriptive (historical) is to fall prey to the kind of criticisms just mentioned. There is also the danger of placing an unbalanced emphasis on the parahistorical. As he states:

... it would be facile to think of religious ideas as existing just in people's heads or on paper. They can only be properly understood in their living milieu. Thus Christian theology has to be seen in its institutional and sacramental environment. It has to do with faith, with people, with worship. It is not just a piece of metaphysics, and not a free-floating ideology.

[Smart 1968: 15]

In fact 'religious ideas are not just ideas but *religious* ideas' (Smart 1968: 15).

So although the educational aim is 'the production of a ripe capacity to judge the truth of what is propagated,' (Smart 1968: 97) it is important that students develop and exercise 'skilful sensitivity' (Smart 1968: 95), which the phenomenological epoch (suspension of judgement) and empathy was designed to help bring about. 'People are free not to believe or respond to Christian or Buddhist ideas. But before there can be response, there should be comprehension. Before rejection, there should be sensitivity' (Smart 1968: 103).

So at its best phenomenological religious education would seek to delineate and integrate the historical and parahistorical (to use Smart's terminology) or the practices and beliefs and truth claims of religion (to use, perhaps, simpler terminology); something, which has not always been achieved successfully in religious education.

Activity

Do you use or have you used the phenomenological approach? If so, how? How do you respond to the criticism that this approach merely describes religion to students rather than engaging them in critical thinking? Does your teaching enable them to think critically? If so, how do you ensure that?

Comment: implicit and explicit phenomenological approaches to RE

During the 1970s there grew up a distinction between what was referred to as *implicit religious education* and *explicit religious education*. This distinction was partly to do with work of Ronald Goldman and Harold Loukes but it also had theological underpinnings, arising out of a stream of liberal Christian theology. This originally manifested itself on the continent of Europe in the work of such notable theologians as Bultmann, Bonhoeffer and Tillich and reached this country with the seminal work of the then Bishop of Woolwich, John Robinson, in his work *Honest to God*.

Bultmann was famous for his notion of *demythologizing* – the idea that the world of ideas surrounding the writers of the New Testament had to be reinterpreted in order for it to make sense to twentieth-century people. Tillich saw religion as that which deals with the ultimate concerns of people (for example issues to do with death and the meaning of life) and secondary to this, doctrines and ideologies.

Towards the end of the 1970s Smart wrote an article, 'What is Religion?' – printed in his book, *New Movements in Religious Education* – which set out the theoretical understandings for the implicit/explicit divide.

Smart distinguishes between different types of question. He categorizes a question such as, 'Why do Muslims go on pilgrimages to Mecca?' as an example of a *question about a religion*. A *religious question*, according to Smart, is one that concerns matters of profound human concern, namely, 'Why do people suffer?' or 'What lies beyond death?' It is these questions of ultimate concern: questions to do with meaning, value and purpose, that should lie at the heart of religious education. This, of course, is not to say that the other type of question to do with religious phenomena is not important.

In the development of religious education such distinctions were taken to inform the implicit and the explicit approaches to teaching religious education.

Implicit religious education concerned students' own *experiences, feelings, emotions, and insights*, both within him/herself and with relationships between people. By concentrating on these things it was hoped that students may begin to be sensitive towards and ask questions about human experience in order to understand this at depth.

The *explicit* dimension or approach to religious education concentrated on *aspects of the phenomenon of religion as an observable fact* within the world. In practice this often involved a concentration on aspects such as festivals, food, pilgrimages, sacred books, founders of religions, etc.

The influence of Michael Grimmitt

These two dimensions were worked out in full by Michael Grimmitt in his influential work of the mid-1970s, *What Can I Do in RE?*

Grimmitt constructed a two-part conceptual framework consisting of the *existential approach* and the *dimensional approach* (Grimmitt 1973: 49–113). These were developments from the *Schools Council Working Paper 36* (1971), which introduced the terms implicit and explicit religious education.

There are several key aspects of this approach that are worth highlighting. First, the approach recognizes that religious education involves helping pupils become informed about religion through developing accurate religious concepts. However, if, as Grimmitt insists, a student's thinking is developmental, then religious education should also be developmental. Such an approach 'demands that a child's own experiences, needs and interests become the starting point for learning' (Grimmitt 1973: 47). As Grimmitt stated when discussing his two approaches, 'Ideally a teacher should ensure that these two approaches are used in combination with each other as they are complementary.' (Grimmitt 1973: 51)

While the work of Grimmitt in the 1970s, and of the Schools Council, helped religious education make great strides in curriculum development, some consequences of the implicit/explicit approach were unfortunate. Themes such as 'caring' in the primary school and 'marriage' in the secondary school, whilst dealing with important aspects of human experience, did so with little or no reference to religions. In the most extreme examples, it was possible to imagine that the removal of religious education from the curriculum would make little or no difference to what went on. Such themes as above could quite easily be embraced by a subject called social studies or personal, social and moral education.

Lastly, any concentration on the explicit tended to do so in a way that divorced the study of religion from the concerns of human experience. There was a danger of explicit religious education becoming a collection of strange customs and observances that bore little relevance and relationship to children's own existential concerns.

What was needed was an approach that recognized the importance of both dimensions but in practice included them both.

Religious education and human development: an instrumental approach

Nevertheless, the integrative dimension to Grimmitt's work took a major step forward with the publication in 1987 of his book *Religious Education and Human Development*. This contains a detailed rationale for the human development approach to religious education. According to Grimmitt, the structure of the curriculum should be designed to enable pupils to develop the skills and abilities required to apply insights gained from their study of religion to an understanding of their own situations and experiences (Grimmitt 2000: 20). Importantly, such a curriculum only includes content from religions that illuminate and inform the student about human experience. These would include areas such as: order, meaning and purpose in the universe and truth, questions about human nature, a just society, individual self-fulfilment and ethical issues, as well as questions about the nature of community and values.

Such pedagogical principles illustrate Grimmitt's conviction that the study of religion should play an *instrumental* role in the pedagogy of religious education. What is important for the learner is not knowledge of religion *per se* but the way in which a religious believer perceives the world and how these insights can inform how the learner sees the world.

Learning about and learning from religion

Central to this is the pedagogical procedure or strategy of learning about and from religion. These terms have since become axiomatic in religious education featuring in the SCAA Model Syllabuses (1994) and, most recently, in the *Non-Statutory National Framework for Religious Education* (2004).

Pause for reflection

What do you understand by the terms learning about and learning from religion? Can you define each term?

Comment

Grimmitt's original vision of the educational value of studying religion was that it should involve a study of the central concepts of religion, illustrated by references to different religions, but, as noted above, not a study of the different religions for their own sake.

According to Grimmitt *learning from religion* involves students in evaluating what they have learnt about religion in both impersonal and personal terms. Impersonal evaluation involves 'being able to distinguish and make critical evaluations of truth claims, beliefs and practices of different religious traditions and of religion itself' (Grimmitt 1987: 225). Such an evaluation may include the ability to make distinctions between expressions of religion that promote human flourishing and those expressions that are antithetical to such flourishing. So for Grimmitt, personal evaluation 'begins as an attempt to confront and evaluate religious beliefs and values [and] becomes a process of self-evaluation' (Grimmitt 1987: 26). In addition, we would want to stress, more strongly than Grimmitt, that such personal evaluation might also include an application of what students can learn from religion in order for them to develop a critical view of the world around them.

We noted above that Ofsted, in particular, have been critical of some teaching using the learning about religion and learning from religion model. Such criticisms largely lie in the identification of poor practice in terms of what students are learning about. We have noted that often this involves undemanding descriptive teaching. It is important for us to take such criticisms into account when outlining the approach that informs this book.

Spirituality in religious traditions

We discussed in Chapter 2 the idea of a spiritual side to science. The question for us here is what might a spiritual interpretation of religion look like? This is an important question if the study of religion is to be understood as having the potential to make a distinctive contribution to the curriculum.

There are many ways to study religion and there are many different definitions of religion. In the professional world of religious education the study of religion has been firmly located in the move away from a theological approach to a multi-dimensional approach as understood by the discipline of religious studies. So religion can be studied from an historical, sociological or psychological point of view, for example. Whilst many religious educators today will not see a problem with this, one can still ask the question, if the kind of Christian education that predated modern approaches to the subject attempted to enable students to understand the world from a Christian point of view, what is to understand the world from a broadly religious point of view? We think it is a question worth asking because if there is something distinctive about a religious view of experience, our pupils should be enabled to understand it. But how does one conceptualize this?

Several modern writers – for example, John Hick, Keith Ward and Karen Armstrong – have argued that what is distinctive of what are often called post-axial religions (roughly the period from 900–200 BCE when the great religious traditions were formed, teaching a spiritual ethic of love, compassion and non-violence) is that human responses to the transcendent are soteriological in character. Religions are thus concerned, 'with the transformation of the self through an appropriate response to that which is most truly real' (Ward 1987: 153).

Human transformation in the world's religions

What follows in this section of the chapter is a brief summary based on key concepts from the six 'major' religious traditions, which illustrate understandings about human nature and its transformation.

Whilst religious traditions are varied and complex it is possible to identify certain clusters of distinctive concepts that encompass a religion's soteriological dimension.

Human transformation may be understood in two dimensions. First, all the 'major' religions conceive of *human nature* and experience as being essentially unsatisfactory. Indeed this is the meaning of the Buddhist term *dukkha*. Second, because humans are subject to *tanha* (craving) life is never satisfactory. We crave for that which we do not possess which leads to a constant experience of life as less than satisfactory. This human experience is caused by our spiritual blindness or *avidya*. This spiritual blindness is the first link in the chain of causes of human suffering, referred to as the doctrine of dependent origination.

Avidya is a key concept that underpins other indigenous religious traditions of India such as Hinduism and Sikhism. In Hinduism *avidya* leads to *maya* (illusion about that which is truly real) leading to attachment to the world of *samsara*.

For Sikhs *avidya* and *maya* cause the condition known as *haumai*, which means ego or I-centredness. A person who is subject to *haumai* is known as *manmukh*.

According to Guru Nanak it is *haumai* that controls unregenerate man to such an extent that 'human beings are inexorably bound to the wheel of transmigration'.

In the Semitic traditions of Judaism, Christianity and Islam this unsatisfactoriness is understood largely in moral terms. In human nature there is a tendency to 'fall away' from God. In Christianity it is through 'falleness' caused by the sin of the first human beings in the Garden of Eden. This causes human beings to live a life alienated from God.

In Judaism, whilst there is no conception of 'original sin' human beings are created with free will, with its constant tension between our evil inclination, *yetzer ha-ra*, and good inclination, *yetzer ha-tov*.

In Islam, although human beings are created with the capacity to understand and live by the absolute qualities of God, such as mercy, compassion and love, our earthly existence with its need for survival often causes us to be weak and fallible – hence the tendency to be subject to 'forgetfulness of God' or *ghafala*.

The religious traditions provide, for human beings, a vision and a path of a limitlessly better life conceived in quite radically different ways in which human beings may achieve liberation from, and *transformation* of, a self centred and unsatisfactory existence. Religions provide a means by which humans may become liberated from such unsatisfactory dimensions of the human condition.

For the Buddhist this consists of understanding the four noble truths: following the eightfold path and five precepts in a path of meditation and 'skilful living', developing the qualities of *metta* (loving kindness) and *karuna* (compassion) leading to the state of *nibbana*.

For Hindus, spirituality and daily life are inseparable. There are a variety of spiritual paths, or yogas: *bhakti yoga* (devotion), *jnana yoga* (spiritual insight and knowledge), *raja yoga* (meditation) and *karma yoga* (selfless service). These paths are not necessarily tightly compartmentalized but in their various ways lead the devotee to spiritual liberation (*moksha*).

For the Sikh following a path of *nam simran* (keeping God constantly in mind) and *sewa* (selfless service) and hence developing *gurmukh* (God-centredness) leads to a state of *mukhti*.

For Jews the *halakhah* (Jewish religious law) provides the link between human beings and God. Mystical Judaism contains the idea of *tikkun olam*, whereby creation caused disunity in the world and divine sparks were scattered throughout the universe. Thus humanity's task is to repair the world and for the Jew that means bringing *kedusha* (God's holiness) into the world through the development of harmonious relationships with fellow human beings and with God.

The Christian understanding of salvation is that although the human condition is a distortion of its true nature, God is at work in the world bringing individuals and indeed the whole of creation to its true destiny. What is distinctively Christian about this view of human nature is that most Christians believe that the salvation of humankind has been achieved by the death and resurrection of Jesus Christ. Thus humans can achieve redemption through faith in Jesus Christ and by the development of what St Paul calls the 'fruits of the spirit'.

Obedience to the will of Allah for a Muslim through religious practice based on the *shariah* and the inward spirituality of *tariqah* develops the virtues of an Islamic personality leading to paradise.

So on this interpretation of religion what is common between the religions is that they provide the means for humans to transcend incompleteness and achieve spiritual liberation. There is no suggestion, however, that these various views about human nature and destiny are essentially the same. Each religion differs as to what is the human spiritual defect and in the spiritual path of transformation, and as to the goal to which this path eventually leads. Nevertheless, what they have in common is this soteriological function. While different from each other, they share similar patterns of interpretation of human nature and how it can be transformed.

There are, of course, other ways to interpret religion but we would argue that this particular framework enables students to understand religion and science as related – yet distinct – disciplines that can enable students to widen and deepen their understanding of both what lies at the heart of the religions and science and their interpretation of the human condition.

The approach that informs this book

We have suggested in our overview of religious education pedagogy that the phenomena and teachings of religions are not just to be studied for their own sake, but as means by which students may expand and deepen their understanding of the human experience.

In Chapter 5 we outline our pedagogical approach to learning in religion and science, which we refer to as 'skilfully learning'. This refers to a Buddhist term *upaya*, or 'skilful means'. This was a concept used by the

Buddha in two ways. First, religious teachers, such as Jesus or the Buddha, used metaphor, parable, etc. to communicate spiritual truths to their followers. It is possible to conceive of the religious educator using *upaya* in this sense but with the concern that his or her approach may be bordering on the confessional. However, the use of the term *upaya* in a second sense can best be described by the Buddha's famous parable of the raft. Briefly, a man comes to a river that has no bridge or means of crossing so he constructs a raft from reeds and branches. He then uses the raft to paddle to the other side. Because the raft has been useful he is tempted to take it with him on his journey. The Buddha counters against this, suggesting the man leave the raft behind. The raft was a 'skilful means' by which the man could continue on his journey. In the Buddha's teaching the raft stands for the *dharma*.

It is in this second sense that religious education might be understood as *upayic*. We are not suggesting that you, as a teacher, present religions to students as 'skilful means'. That would be to prioritize Buddhist understanding over any other. Rather the religions, understood as vehicles of human transformation, can operate within the teaching and learning process as 'skilful means' by which the students develop a wider and deeper understanding of what it means to be human. There is no intention that students carry any particular religion with them on their journey, although they may of course already have a religion. If this is the case then learning about and from other religious traditions may enrich the tradition to which they already belong. For students of no religious adherence insights from the various religions may enrich their own particular stance on life, or even assist them in developing one. This is a two-way process by which students might use what they learn about and from religion as a critical filter when considering the world in which they are growing up. It is two-way because their experience of growing up in a western democracy will require them to explore religious teachings and practices critically on the basis of their own developing beliefs and values.

As mentioned above we explore this approach more fully in Chapters 5 and 6, which together form the basis of our approach to the example lesson plans in Chapters 7 and 8.

Further reading

Everington, J. (2000) 'Mission Impossible? Religious Education in the 1990s' in Leicester, M., Mogdil, C. & Mogdil S., *Spiritual and Religious Education*. London: Falmer Press.

Grimmitt, M. (1973) *What Can I Do in RE?* Great Wakering, Essex: McCrimmons.

Grimmitt, M. (1987) *Religious Education and Human Development: The Relationship Between Studying Religions and Personal, Social and Moral Education*. Great Wakering, Essex: McCrimmons.

Grimmitt, M. (2000) *Pedagogies of Religious Education: Case Studies in the Research and Development of Good Pedagogic Practice in RE*. Great Wakering Essex: McCrimmons.

Hick, J. (1966) *Faith and Knowledge*, 2nd edn. Glasgow: Collins Fount Paperbacks.

Hick, J. (1999) *The Fifth Dimension: An Exploration of the Spiritual Realm*. Oxford: One World.

Hick, J. (2004) *An Interpretation of Religion: Human Responses to the Transcendent*, 2nd edn. London: Macmillan.

Qualifications and Curriculum Authority (2004) *Religious Education: The Non-Statutory National Framework*. London: QCA & DfES.

Read, G., Rudge, J., Teece, G. & Howarth, R. B. (1992) *How Do I Teach RE? The Westhill Project Religious Education 5–16*, 2nd edn. Cheltenham: Stanley Thornes.

School Curriculum and Assessment Authority (1994) *Model Syllabuses for Religious Education*: Model 1: Living Faiths Today; Model 2: Questions and Teachings. London: SCAA.

Schools Council Working Paper No. 36 (1971) *Religious Education in Secondary Schools*. London: Evans/Methuen.

Smart, N. (1968) *Secular Education and the Logic of Religion*. London: Faber and Faber.

Cantwell Smith, W. (1978) *The Meaning and End of Religion: A New Approach to the Religious Traditions of Mankind*. London, SPCK.

Ward, K. (1987) *Images of Eternity*. London: Darton, Longman & Todd.

Part 2

Pedagogy in practice

Chapter 5

Teaching religion and science themes

Chapter overview

In this chapter we will explore the main themes that lie at the heart of teaching religion and science and the issues you will need to address when teaching religious and scientific notions of truth, explanation, meaning and purpose. We will then show you how you can put into practice the notion of 'skilful means' introduced in Chapter 4 to allow your students to develop the skills they'll need to act as 'critical filters' when learning about religion and science.

Issues of truth

Addressing possible preconceptions and misconceptions

Should a person's religious belief automatically exclude them from using scientific explanations? If not, how does any individual accommodate what, may appear to others to be irreconcilable authorities for our reasoning and decisions, our actions and behaviour? Such questions lie at the heart of the individual differences you'll encounter when teaching religion and science; not just when exploring the obviously more contentious issues – the focus of the next chapter – but also when you focus on 'everyday' topics where science impinges on our decisions and actions, such as: healthcare, consumerism, or the impact of new technologies.

Most professional scientists would say that they do not *believe* in evolutionary theory; its use is not based on a leap of faith. Instead scientists *accept* evolutionary theory as the best scientific explanation currently available based on a systematic evaluation of the evidence. Understanding the distinction between *belief* in a scientific construct in the absence of objective evidence, and an *acceptance* that is based on an evaluation of the evidence, is crucial for an accurate appreciation of the nature of scientific knowledge's development.

When helping your students to learn from religion and science, they may automatically comprehend new information and initially accept it, but will only reject it in cases where they have sufficient opportunity, motivation, or previous information to evaluate the claim. An example of a topic where your students' own views might well undergo significant belief shifts as different issues are explored is the study of illness and suffering (see Chapter 8). By investigating historical examples such as plague or leprosy, or more contemporary illnesses such as smallpox, or AIDS, your students will be able to explore such questions as: can affliction with a disease be seen as a punishment for past sins or actions (the biblical Ten Plagues)? How might the concept of suffering be reconciled with the notion of a loving God or the death of 'innocent' children? What role should science play in 'preventing' hereditary disease, the 'screening' of embryos or altering 'God's design'? Students are able to learn about how religious and scientific views of disease affect our understanding of, and reaction to, illness and their impact on our beliefs, actions and choices. Your role is, therefore, to enable students to construct their own coherent explanation as to why they accept or reject, retain or dismiss a particular viewpoint.

The challenge for you is that the information you present (such as an evolutionary explanation of human origins) may exist 'in limbo' – not being considered strictly true in the same sense as other (perhaps faith- or culturally-based) beliefs – but still being used by your students: to be recalled, retrieved and presented in assessments, such as exams, and used to support inferential processes. Such information may, ultimately, be incorporated in individual students' wider explanatory models (e.g. in shaping their attitude as an adult to environmental taxation) and so also be used in the service of further inferences.

The efficacy of any teaching and learning will depend, however, upon the extent to which the information presented is compatible with your students' spontaneous assumptions. One such is the view that hearing, visual or physical impairments are negative 'disabilities' that should be prevented or removed. Any information you provide that violates earlier developed principles – the views of Jehovah's Witnesses on medical intervention – might well trigger a degree of scepticism. Such testimonies could be viewed by your students as 'unimportant' because the rationale for such views may have few discernable links to most students' day-to-day assumptions. In contrast, some testimonies – such as deaf parents 'preferring' to have deaf children, or Roman Catholic Christian views on the 'rights' of the foetus – may be seen as significant because they make the information content especially dramatic and memorable.

On whose authority?

So, if you invite your students to reflect on beliefs that do not match their initial spontaneous assumptions – and, as in the examples given above, are often described in ways that are emotionally counterintuitive – it may not be a coincidence that your suggestions arouse reactions from your students that are antagonistic or distrustful, or are immediately rejected. The inculcation of cultural and/or religious knowledge, norms, and concepts generally involves particularly authoritative figures whose statements are supposedly more reliable or closer to the truth than those of average members of a community or believers. Furthermore, when discussing issues where knowledge directly affects behaviour, the authoritativeness of a source (e.g. a scientific study) as a cue of reliability often seems very weak compared with early acquired, personal, religious or cultural experiences. As a student's knowledge about a topic increases – such as when we explore biological evolutionary theory – the acceptance of novel, contradictory or unexpected information on that topic becomes less likely. In contrast, information is accepted quite readily if the student has little or no previous knowledge, or if the information does not seem to contradict previously existing knowledge (for example, a genetic explanation of heredity).

What do we believe?

The very conditional nature of scientific knowledge – which, for many professional scientists is one of its greatest strengths – is perversely, for some students, its greatest weakness. The constructivist's view insists that the knowledge of evolution is science's best reckoning of reality. It is what science accepts and what scientists currently view as the most valid interpretation of phenomena. Of critical importance here is that constructed knowledge admits to doubt and does not carry the force of truth. Knowing is accepting that such-and-such is so, which raises the question of why one concept makes sense and is acceptable to one person but not to another person? The answer lies outside the classroom, for the knowledge constructions by which we make sense of the world are influenced by culturally situated fundamental beliefs that are not easily changed.

In Chapter 3 we showed how individual differences in the way we use religion and science to make sense of the world affects the relative value we give to different types of information. Those students who accept religious knowledge as immutable but scientific knowledge as changeable often find it perfectly logical to favour the former over the latter. Such students also only tend to accept as 'believable' scientific laws with high levels of certainty and are sceptical of theories that may be postulated to understand their underlying processes. This is because laws are more directly observable – you can undertake measurements and 'see' the laws governing ecological systems in action – but where is the direct evidence for proof of the evolutionary theories that might explain the behaviour of individual species? For such students, theories that explain observable phenomena are proven hypotheses that can become laws when they become confirmed, or are hypotheses that have been supported over a long period of time. Such students may also hold the mistaken notion that those theories that are consistently supported by experimentation and observation become accepted laws. This is because most students make skewed judgements about what evidence is valid (direct) and what is not (historical and circumstantial). Furthermore, they want to subject historical evidence to 'tests' that are only appropriate for direct evidence, reflecting a misunderstanding of the nature of different types of evidence and how they relate to one another. Such scepticism is not, however, reserved for ideas that might conflict with religious views such as Big Bang and evolution. Ideas – like the black hole explanation of quasars or stellar evolution – are equally likely to be dismissed, where the personal relevance of the event appears to bear only a remote connection to answering the questions *that matter* to the student.

Issues regarding explanations

Ideas: are they static or evolving?

You (and your students) might well be unsettled by science's apparent objectivity and the fact that the explanations offered by science do not seem to be open to critique or scepticism. Certainly most of us would admit that much of the corpus of scientific data is not contentious. However, what does and continues to change is the framework through which that information is understood, appreciated and explained, and the scientific models developed to frame explanations and utilize sets of ideas. Specifically, scientists assess whether a particular model can explain the data at hand and predict the results of future experiments. They also evaluate how well a model fits with other accepted models as well as other types of knowledge.

Most crucially, once constructed, models influence and constrain the kinds of questions we ask about the world and the types of evidence we seek in support of particular arguments. They guide a questioner's perception of what is involved in the natural processes of the world. A clear example of a shift in perception is how in many countries the public attitude to tobacco smoking has altered over the last 60 years as knowledge of the biological effects of tobacco have become understood amongst the general population.

Of course, people's religious ideas have also changed and developed over time. For example, Karen Armstrong has traced developing ideas about God in the Semitic traditions in her 1994 book *A History of God*, while John Hick's *An Interpretation of Religion* mentions how the Christian image of God has changed over the centuries: in medieval Europe, God was imaged and experienced as a remote and terrifying power to be dreaded, while in modern times the concept is of a God of limitless love incarnate in Jesus.

The need for certainty

Those of your students who are not readily convinced by scientific arguments are, in effect, expressing their criteria for proof. Because these students believe that scientific knowledge changes (progresses?) in ways that religious knowledge does not, what they are actually seeking is the same level of certainty from scientific arguments as they attribute to their religious beliefs. For a proof to be adequate for these students, it should, at the very best, be able to be personally experienced or, at the very least, be personally meaningful.

Issues to do with meaning and purpose

To appreciate how and why issues of a scientific nature impact on religious thinking, you will need to capture in some form and offer to your students the meaningful goals for science, and the day-to-day ends towards which scientists work. These are to be found and understood in the local context of practice, the nature of which varies from scientific discipline to discipline and even from one research question to the next. For example, a neurologist might focus on understanding how the human brain is organized to perceive the colour and shape of objects and their meanings, but might have no insight into the symbolism used in Christian iconography or the representations of Hindu deities. In other words, most scientists occupy themselves trying to understand only how selected, highly circumscribed portions of the world work, not with developing a coherent picture of the world as a whole.

Pause for reflection

What picture do you have of the professional scientist? What are the meanings and purposes of their work? How does it compare to your view of the professional teacher or religious leader?

Comment: scientists as people

In your discussions surrounding the process and procedures of science, your students may often refer to 'scientists' rather than 'science', as if the 'scientists' represent 'science'; its explanations and accounts. Is this the same as you or your colleagues representing all that is good or bad about the educational system, or the Imam representing all that is good or bad about Islam? Certainly our perception of science, education or religion is tempered by our direct experiences and our vicarious exposure to its products through the media. Of these three professions, 'scientist' is the one that is most likely the least accessible to direct personal experience by your students.

As in most areas of human endeavour, science is often laborious and repetitive. Developments in science do, and should, alter the way we perceive and interact with the natural world, but the individual scientist's role is mostly as part of a greater, collaborative endeavour. Contrast this to the dramatic transformations that the same individual scientist might experience in their personal life when coming face-to-face with an inspirational teacher or a charismatic priest, and the meanings they will attach to the events they thus witness and experience.

As we have already seen in Chapters 2 and 3, the role played by science in an individual's understanding of issues varies. There are working scientists who are atheists, agnostics and humanists, whereas others are also 'people of faith' – some even ordained religious priests. How they, you, or we respond to science and religion issues will be as a human being rather than as a practitioner of a certain profession.

Acting on our values and beliefs

If you were to ask your students to describe the relationship between science and religion, how would you know if they were describing their own views or the views they associate with science and/or religion? For example, a student may trust the expertise of medical doctors. However, for explaining something as remarkable as living, breathing creatures, capable of comprehending the world around them and themselves, that same student might not want to rely on what the scientists say but may also want to look for truth from authorities that 'speak to them' in terms that makes sense of their personal life experiences and history.

If not their religious outlook, a student's aesthetic values may similarly provoke an individual to object to scientific practices – Lewis Wolpert's 'yuck factor' – that exposes science's mode of working in a personally objectionable way. For example, from the apparently instrumentalist view of the human body of much medical research – whether it be the unlawful removal of body organs from cadavers, or the lack of sanctity shown to foetuses that might be aborted or used in stem cell therapies – science could be seen as reducing humans to unthinking, unfeeling biological machines.

For students wary of science's apparent 'soullessness', such a view of science violates an image of the world their beliefs and values affords them. As we will show later, your role is, therefore, to allow your students to understand what might be the basis for the attitudes they hold, to appreciate why alternate positions might be argued and the basis for these alternative views and what skills they will need to use to make sense of their own position and those of others.

Religion and science as meaning makers

Where do we find meaning?

Is it easy to distinguish between a person for whom religious faith matters and a person who is convinced of the importance of scientific explanations in understanding the world we inhabit? The person of religion is thought to have a particular and characteristic mode of existence in the world; they accept that life has a sacred origin that has an absolute reality that transcends the world but is capable of being experienced in the world. In contrast, the irreligious person refuses transcendence and believes that all life is relative and may even come to doubt that life has any ultimate meaning. Such a person aims to 'demystify' life and, to them, the idea of God and any accompanying moral and sacred demands are a limit on human freedom.

What would be interesting is to see where the basis of our ability to identify with either of these images comes from? Is anyone wholly religious as they go about their everyday lives?

Activity

To whom would you turn to help you gain an understanding of the issues concerning:

- the promotion and use of nuclear energy?
- the promotion and use of genetic screening?
- the promotion and use of social networking communications?

What gave them the authority they required to be credible? Was it:

- their academic, religious and/or scientific credentials?
- their ability to communicate the issues in a way that you could comprehend?
- the fact that they shared your values and concerns?

Comment: finding one's voice

What is interesting to ask is what role do you think you play when imparting information to your students? Are you in danger of being perceived as a 'mouthpiece' for the views of others, or are you helping your students to develop the capacity (as described in Chapter 4) – a voice to use and respond to the information we give them – to transform themselves?

With the pressures you already have, is it even fair for us to ask you to do more; to explore and develop in your students their voice to express what the interaction between religion and science *means to them*?

We believe that by helping your students to work in this way you will also be helping them to use what they have learnt from studying religion and science issues as 'critical filters' when studying religion in general, as your students will have internalized a set of criteria from which to make judgements of others' and their own developing opinions.

These critical filters are achieved through you fostering the transformative, aesthetic experiences of your students. Whilst they are engaged learning, they are also applying what they learn to situations they face outside. The study of religion and science therefore becomes a means by which individuals can seek answers for themselves; to test their ideas and those of others, to assuage their curiosity and so be the impetus for further learning.

Skilfully learning from the study of religion and science

We have already introduced in Chapter 4 the notion of 'skilful means', by which students can develop a wider and deeper understanding of what it means to be human, as our pedagogical solution to the challenge of teaching students about both religion and science. In this section we will explore how this approach can be put into practice to enable your students to learn from the issues they study. How you might address specific, challenging topics in the curriculum will be discussed in the next chapter.

There are three interlinked aspects in our approach to how your students can learn from the study of religion and science (see diagram). Taken together they form the skilful means by which students wonder as to how they should *reflect on*, *engage with* and *illuminate* their understanding of religion and science.

Using the above learning approach your students will be able to reflect on what are the beliefs and values they hold dear and why. If some of your students feel their values and beliefs are threatened by a scientific world view, introducing them to multiple theoretical explanations for a single phenomenon will allow them to engage with the issues in a way that is both purposeful and meaningful. Helping your students explore the limitations and implications of the different scientific and religious perspectives will illuminate what types of argument can help them understand their own responses, but what are also useful ways to understand responses different to their own. The learning cycle is then repeated because in the process of engaging with alternative viewpoints, the opportunity is opened up for the student to transcend and develop a modified view of their own, as the student allows these alternate perspectives to inform their own understanding.

make impersonal
observations of how
specific religious
principles determine
responses to particular
R&S issues. So students
can develop critical
filters to illuminate and
inform their personal
perspective. To ...

enable students to
reflect on their emotional
response to R&S issues.
Use this to form the
basis of their view of the
world around them. So
that they can critically ...

use their personal
experiences to engage
with specific R&S
issues, rather than
examine the topic in the
abstract or through
someone else's
perspective. So that they
can then ....

So, for example, when in Chapter 8 we explore Darwinian evolutionary theory, this approach will give your students the tools to engage with
the issues in a way that is both purposeful and meaningful but not overtly
threatening. It will also help you to understand how *your* students may vary
in the ways they explore the Darwinian evolutionary model and highlight
what types of argument will help *them*.

Further reading

Cobern, W. W. (2000) *Everyday Thoughts about Nature*. Dordrecht, The
Netherlands: Kluwer Academic Publishers.

This book tries to find out how (American) secondary school-aged students and their science teachers 'think about Nature or the natural world, and how their thoughts are related to science'.

Dear, P. (2006) *The Intelligibility of Nature: How Science Makes Sense of the World*. Chicago: University of Chicago Press.
This book focuses on an historical exploration of 'how science has evolved and positioned itself' and, ultimately, the professionalization of its proponents.

Midgley, M. (1995) *Beast and Man: The Roots of Human Nature*. Oxford: Routledge.
This book explores some of the philosophical questions surrounding human nature and our similarities and differences to other species.

Trigg, R. (1999, Second edition) *Ideas of Human Nature: An Historical Introduction*. Oxford: WileyBlackwell.
This book presents the views of 12 Western thinkers (including Plato, Aquinas, Hume, Darwin and Freud) on human nature and discusses their relevance to contemporary controversies.

Chapter 6

Teaching controversial topics

Chapter overview

In this chapter we explore the specific challenges you will face when addressing controversial issues. Following the pedagogical approach we have described in previous chapters, we detail some 'ground rules' that should minimize some of the potential drawbacks you might encounter when teaching these topics, we then show you how to get the most out of exploring such topics in your lessons.

Pause for reflection

What, for you, are examples of 'controversial issues'? What would you describe as the main characteristics of a 'controversial issue'? What makes it so, and why?

The characteristics of controversy

There are three characteristics of an issue that Ralph Levinson has highlighted as being present, and thought of as 'controversial', when:

- people start from different premises and hold different key beliefs, understandings and values deriving from the premises
- it involves a substantial number of people or different groups

- the issue is not capable of being settled by appeal to evidence.
  [Taken from: Ralph Levinson (2006) 'Towards a Theoretical
  Framework for Teaching Controversial Socio-scientific Issues',
  International Journal of Science Education, 2810: 1201–1224]

As we have illustrated in the previous chapter, there are numerous difficulties with the pre-suppositions that underpin all three of these characteristics, some or all of which you might well meet with when looking at religion and science issues with your students. Some of the difficulties are:

- Students cannot easily articulate how their views are different from those of others – even when they are in disagreement!
- Differences are not recognized by contending parties as such.
- Students do not share their disagreements or alternative viewpoints. Consensus is only apparent, or the more vocal proponents hold sway in discussions.
- Alternative viewpoints are not given the opportunity to be voiced and/ or heard.
- A stated viewpoint may be viewed as wrong and possibly offensive by others, perhaps for a variety of different reasons which are not shared by all opponents.
- The evidence produced in class has little or no impact on the views of individuals – perhaps due to their indifference or their already developed world view.
- Opinions expressed by students are only temporary, or they are easily persuaded to change their minds when confronted with additional information.

The pedagogical approach we have outlined in the first part of this book is aimed to keep the difficulties you'll meet when teaching controversial issues in religion and science to a minimum. To try to help you to overcome the difficulties in teaching controversial issues listed above, the rest of this chapter is devoted to the ways that you and your students can get the most from exploring such topics.

The teacher's position

Teachers may well feel that adopting a neutral stance – focusing on 'the facts', giving a 'balanced' picture – is most likely to be the 'safest' one to adopt. In practice, this is a very difficult strategy to achieve. The choice of facts you present (or withhold), the 'expert' opinions you share with your students and all the other educational judgments – in terms of the resources chosen and time devoted to the issue being explored – makes the effort of teaching religion and science issues in this way unrealistic. As with all controversial issues, however, your students need to be taught to examine critically the information they are given and the attitudes or values that have led to its production. So, rather than seeking to 'not get involved', you should be explicit about the aims and objectives of any exercise so that your students are aware of the circumstances in which they are being asked for their opinions and share the basis for their thinking. Such a proactive approach – framing the discussion, challenging uncontested assertions – is also beneficial if your students all hold very similar views, thus limiting the diversity of responses that can be obtained via elicitation or student discussion.

Another problem is the tendency for a small number of students to express their views forcefully, thereby discouraging other students from expressing contrary views. Your increased involvement in highly charged discussions might well therefore be appreciated – and necessary – to prevent them from being dominated by a few forthright students, and to maintain the lesson's focus.

Activity

Do any of the following comments reflect your own opinions on the relevance of Darwinian evolution? How might you respond to those views that markedly differ from your own?

The heyday of Darwinism has passed. What is happening is that the secular atheists, who have hijacked science for their own ends are being found out.

Students are likely to be exposed to proponents of creationism and intelligent design. It is essential they understand the historical context and the flaws in the arguments these groups put forward.

You should be worried about what your students are being taught. The whole of creation is groaning in the decay of Adam.

I don't feel it's my place to replace what their families or churches have taught them. There's a lot of confusion about where the line is, and how much it's okay to offend your students.

Teaching about evolution is disastrous because if you teach people that they are animals then it is inevitable that they will behave like animals.

I think the reason why evolution is sometimes taught in such a dogmatic way is that biologists are afraid of the 'religious people'.

The student's position

The pedagogical approach used in this book is specifically designed to help your students to challenge or re-evaluate their own attitudes. The challenge is how best to stop your students simply compartmentalizing their scientific and religious understanding and help them to come to grips with both.

Activity

Here are some differing student views that we've collected on the subject of evolution; some or all of which might reflect the opinions' of your students. How might you 'manage' your teaching so that such opinions are heard and addressed?

> To me creationism doesn't deserve any attention, because it doesn't make any sense. It says that scientific knowledge is incomplete and that there's no way to bridge the gap, which is sort of saying that science should stop trying to find explanations for things.
>
> It seems perfectly natural to me to mix science and faith. Many of us are frustrated by the arrogance of our science teachers ... there must be an alternative that puts God squarely back at the centre of things.
>
> I think a lot of students go through a period of being very conflicted about their faith, especially if they have an innate interest in science. They've so identified their faith with a particular view of what creation means, that it becomes an all-or-nothing kind of thing. I do think creationism offers an alternative, although I would argue it's not a good one.

What we would like to describe here are two 'ground rules' that will help your students make use of the pedagogical process we've previously described and the teaching strategy outlined in Chapter 5.

Ground rule no. I: 'challenge yourself not others'

- How 'secure' is your position?
- What would need to happen for you to change your position to another one expressed? Why won't this occur?
- What are the strengths and weaknesses of your own position?
- How would you try convincing yourself to change your position?

What is very difficult for students is to be sufficiently objective in their ability to analyse their own position and those of others. Rather, your goal should be to help your students to develop an appreciation that not all problems have a single right answer, although some do; that as science progresses, some of what we once held to be true also changes; and that what on the surface appear to be opposing viewpoints may, in some cases, be synthesized into a new framework. Similarly, an appreciation that an historical understanding of developments in science has parallels with our own developing scientific skills; to enhance one's ability to think critically as well as divergently and to solve ill-structured problems.

Ground rule no. 2: 'tell your story with your own voice'

- Is what you are saying genuinely expressing what you believe, or are you paraphrasing what others might say or think?
- Think carefully about the language and phrases you are using, do they feel strange to say? Are you using language in a way comfortable to you?

There is often a gulf between the issues your students are asked to study and the authoritative scientific accounts and religious orthodoxies they are asked to incorporate into their writings, essays and explanations. Developing their own 'voice' (see also Chapter 5) is a way for students to speak that allows them to relate and listen to the experiences understood or imagined by other parties. It also allows opinions to be recounted where other means constrain such accounts; allowing your students to develop their own 'story' in such a way that it becomes open to *critically* discussing another's ideas and viewpoints.

We are well aware that implementing the pedagogical approach we suggest when teaching a 'controversial' issue such as Darwinian evolutionary theory is not without difficulties and should be introduced gradually. And, as we shall describe in the next two chapters, it should be initially introduced through discussions about the nature of science, focusing on issues where personal attitudes are not seen as a major factor in their acceptance. Then, later, as classroom criteria are established and their necessity appreciated by your students, the rules for future discussions can be agreed; where students with differing attitudes are treated respectfully, thus allowing learning by all to take place.

In terms of the interlinking 'skilful means' described in Chapter 5, students might be first asked to 'use their personal experiences to engage with specific issues' by discussing some of the contemporary Victorian reactions to Darwin's evolutionary theory. Exploring such questions as: 'What arguments might Darwin's supporters use to 'win over' their proponents?' or, 'What counter-arguments could be deployed?' and 'Do any of the issues discussed remain pertinent today?', allow students to elicit a variety of perspectives for themselves without advocating one particular view. Such a procedurally neutral approach would then allow your students to make impersonal observations of how specific religious principles determine responses to particular issues. Thus an historical exploration of the interaction between Darwin's religious and scientific world views (see Chapter 8) could then be used by students to help them gain an appreciation of an individual scientist's response to cultural, social and personal influences on their work.

As we shall discuss more fully in Chapter 8, your students should also be encouraged to compare and contrast the alternate, theoretical approaches available to Darwin and his contemporaries. For example, your students could be asked to discuss the relative merits of Darwin's model of natural selection, Lamarck's model of use inheritance and Paley's model of intelligent design and apply these alternative models to a particular phenomenon and evaluate the success or otherwise of these alternatives explanations. This would help your students to 'reflect on their response' to the fact that Darwin's *Origins* marked a significant change in the way scientist's perceived evolutionary processes. In doing so, your students would have to construct for themselves a narrative explanation which, would not only enable them to appreciate and understand the conceptual issues of the topic under discussion, but it would also provide them with key, alternative world views to compare and contrast with their own. Here is an opportunity for them to 'make impersonal observations' whilst at the same time gaining an appreciation of what were the main theological, as well as scientific challenges, to Darwin's theory in the nineteenth century, and which of these are still relevant today.

Further reading

Hitchens, C. (2008) *God is Not Great: How Religion Poisons Everything.* London: Atlantic Books.

This book aims to be 'the ultimate case against religion'. The book argues that 'the concept of an omniscient God has profoundly damaged humanity', and proposes that 'the world might be a great deal better off without "him"'.

McGrath, A. E. (2005) *The Twilight of Atheism: The Rise and Fall of Disbelief in the Modern World.* London: Rider & Co.

This book purports to show 'what went wrong with the atheist dream' and 'why religion and faith are destined to play a central role in the twenty-first century' by arguing that 'the renewal of faith is a natural, inevitable and necessary response to its failures'.

Park, R. L. (2008) *Superstition: Belief in the Age of Science.* New Jersey: Princeton University Press.

This book reflects on why people persist in superstitious convictions long after 'science has shown them to be ill-founded'. Focusing on supernatural beliefs from religion, the afterlife, New Age spiritualism and faith-based medical claims, the author concludes that 'science is the only way we have of understanding the world'.

Ruse, M. (2004) *Can a Darwinian be a Christian?: The Relationship between Science and Religion.* Cambridge: Cambridge University Press.

This book argues that, although it is at times difficult for a Darwinian to embrace Christian belief, it is by no means inconceivable, and suggests ways in which a Christian believer should have no difficulty accepting evolution in general, and Darwinism in particular.

Chapter 7

Planning lessons for ages 11–16

Chapter overview

This chapter explores how lessons using our pedagogical approach might be planned and taught to students in the lower-secondary age phase (11–16). Teaching objectives are, primarily, taken from England's National Curriculum for religious education – although additional material has been drawn from the Wales' National Exemplar Framework, and Scotland's Curriculum for Excellence – with exemplar lesson plans then showing how the learning objectives could be addressed and how religion and science topics could be used to explore wider religious education concepts. Throughout the chapter, background briefings are included to give a context to the scientific ideas being explored. For more examples of the teaching materials available to support the teaching of religion and science topics, please also refer to the resources detailed in Chapter 1.

What do teachers need to know?

What are the essential skills and processes in religious education that a student needs to learn to make progress? When *learning about religion*, students should be able to:

- investigate the impact of religious beliefs and teachings on individuals, communities and societies, the reasons for commitment and the causes of diversity
- apply a wide range of religious and philosophical vocabulary consistently and accurately, recognizing both the power and limitations of language in expressing religious ideas and beliefs
- explain religious beliefs, practices and commitments, including their transmission by people, texts and traditions
- evaluate how religious beliefs and teachings inform answers to ultimate questions and ethical issues
- interpret a range of sources, texts, authorities, and forms of religious and spiritual expression from a variety of contexts
- analyse religious beliefs, arguments and ideas.

When *learning from religion*, students should be able to:

- reflect on the relationship between beliefs, teachings, world issues and ultimate questions
- evaluate beliefs, commitments and the impact of religious and non-religious perspectives in the contemporary world
- express insights into the significance and value of religion and other world views for human relationships personally, locally and globally
- express their own beliefs and ideas, using a variety of forms of expression, including creative forms and reasoned arguments.

Engagement with religion and science topics, as explored in the exemplar lesson plans below, will enable your students to address all of the above points. As we stated previously, religion and science topics are best explored not in isolation but integrated into your religious education planning as a means of examining the key concepts and principles of religious education. The learning objectives of the exemplar lessons are, therefore, merely illustrative of the pedagogic approach promoted in this book. They are not intended to be 'off the peg' teaching units, but could easily be adapted and extended to fit your particular curriculum planning requirements.

Description of the exemplar lessons

The six lessons explore some of the main issues that are central to the study of religions namely, an examination of our: origins and purpose, views of ourselves, mortality, the physical being and human development. The final lesson draws on the learning that has taken place in the previous lessons, as it explores the generic issue of the veracity that truth claims when examining religious beliefs and practices.

What do students need to know?

The following plans are designed to allow students of differing abilities and maturities to gain from the topics being examined. Your students will need to use their developing religious vocabulary to show their understanding of sources, practices, beliefs, ideas, feelings and experiences, use it to explain the varying impact of beliefs on individuals and communities and explain the reasons for diversity within and between them. They will also need to begin to explain the links between an individual's beliefs and sources of experience, including the interpretations of religious stories and sacred texts, and how these might be used and impact on believers' lives.

Students will then be able to identify questions, and suggests answers, as to what influences them and why. As they make links between aspects of their own and others' experiences, they can then articulate important questions about religion and beliefs: questions of identity, belonging, meaning, purpose and truth. As their ability to make critical links between their own and others' responses develops, they can apply this approach to an exploration of the values and commitments of themselves and others, and their own lives, attitudes and behaviour.

Lesson 1: We are all astronauts on this spaceship earth

This introductory lesson is designed to mirror the unit as whole; namely, to show how explorations of the outer (physical) world might relate to religious ways of making sense of our inner (metaphysical) world and human reasoning of our existence.

The initial focus on an image of planet Earth – devoid of the apparent impact human beings have had on it both structurally and ecologically – is mirrored in the subsequent activity, in which a reflection on the 'importance' of human beings is replaced by consideration of the 'specialness' of the individual and the difficulty in accurately assessing their potential contribution, affect on others and society. The lesson then goes on to explore both Abrahamic and non-theistic religious purposes for human beings. The lesson can then be brought full circle by discussing whether religious explorations can only make sense if human beings are understood as part of (within) the natural world, or special and so set apart.

Key words and phrases

Covenant, God's love, existence, natural theology, self-regard, theology in nature, uniqueness.

Key learning objectives

By the end of the lesson all will:

- know that, for many people, contemplation of our own self-worth raises important questions about our individual origins and purpose.

By the end of the lesson most will:

- reflect on the extent to which human existence provokes questions surrounding the existence of a creator God.

By the end of the lesson some will:

- understand how different religious traditions attempt to understand the relationship between a created being and a creator God.

Concepts

From a religious tradition:

- suggest what meanings might be drawn from responses to. What type of relationship should a created being have with their Creator?

From human experience:

- reflect on the fragility of human existence, our ability to be self-aware and our interactions with others.

From the study of religion:

- investigate what ultimate questions are raised for people about our individual, and collective, roles and purpose.

Background briefing

Captain Jim Lovell graduated from the US Naval Academy, Annapolis in 1952. He became a Navy fighter pilot and then a test pilot. In 1962, he was selected by NASA – the National Aeronautics and Space Administration – to become one of their first astronauts. In 1965 and again in 1966 he went into space aboard a Gemini module, spending almost three weeks orbiting the Earth.

NASA's main aim was to develop a manned vehicle that could leave the Earth's atmosphere and land on the Moon, so keeping the pledge President

Kennedy had made at Rice University on 12 September 1962:

> We choose to go to the moon in this decade, and do . . . other things, not because they are easy but because they are hard, because that goal will serve to organize and measure the best of our energies and skills, because that challenge is one that we are willing to accept, one we are unwilling to postpone, and one which we intend to win.

By 1968 Lovell, William Anders, and Frank Borman were assigned to fly aboard Apollo 8, a dress-rehearsal flight for a lunar landing. Originally they were not scheduled to leave Earth's atmosphere. They were only going to test the slingshot effect – a high-velocity orbit of the Earth that would launch the capsule on a flight to the Moon. However, there were rumors that the Russians were trying to get there first, so NASA changed Apollo 8's flight plan.

Now Apollo 8 would fly to the Moon, orbit around the dark side, and return to Earth in the last week of December. If it all went well, the space-craft would be orbiting the Moon on Christmas Eve, 1968.

On 21 December 1968, Apollo 8 was launched on its 240,000-mile, three-day journey.

Early in the morning on 24 December, Apollo 8 was within reach of the Moon's gravitational pull. The crew fired an engine and manipulated the spacecraft to get into position for a lunar orbit. As Lovell later recounted, 'All of a sudden . . . just sixty-nine miles below, the ancient craters of the far side of the moon were slowly slipping by . . . As we kept going, sud-denly on the lunar horizon, coming up, was Earth.' The contrast between the lifeless Moon and the vibrant Earth was obvious to the astronauts:

> The Moon is nothing but shades of gray and darkness. But the Earth – you could see the deep blues of the seas, the whites of the clouds, the salmon pink and brown of the land masses.

> At one point I sighted the earth with my thumb – and my thumb from that distance fit over the entire planet. I realized how insignificant we all are if everything I'd ever known is behind my thumb. But at that

moment I don't think the three of us understood the lasting significance of what we were looking at:

After a suggestion by NASA, Lovell, Borman and Anders, marked their arrival in Moon orbit by reciting the opening verse of the Bible, from Genesis in the Old Testament:

> In the beginning, God created the heavens and the earth. And the earth was without form, and void; and darkness was upon the face of the deep. And the Spirit of God moved upon the face of the waters. And God said, 'Let there be light'; and there was light. And God saw the light that it was good; and God divided the light from the darkness.
>
> And God called the light Day, and the darkness he called Night.
>
> And God called the dry land Earth; and the gathering of the waters he called Seas; and God saw that it was good.

Lesson structure

1 Opener: display an image of the Earth as seen from space. (e.g. 'Earthrise' as seen from Apollo 8 in 1968; www.apolloarchive.com). Recount the reaction of Apollo 8 Commander, Captain Jim Lovell, when he was able to hide the Earth behind his thumb: 'I realized how insignificant we all are if everything I'd ever known is behind my thumb ... When you see the Earth from the Moon you realize how fragile it is and just how limited the resources are. We are all astronauts on this spaceship Earth.'

2 *Enable students to reflect on their emotional response to issues.* Give each student a copy of a photo (previously taken) in which they have been erased or blacked/cut out. Ask them to think about what is special about themselves? What might be lost (in general) if they had never existed (their *potential* contribution)?

   Plenary: highlight specific and general issues that are raised. For example: lost generations, creative/sporting endeavours; spiritual and religious contributions; memories and influence on the lives of others.

Use their personal experiences to engage with specific issues. Ask students to record individual achievements (past, present and future) using role-play, written, aural or pictorial recordings. For example: Create your own '*This Would Have Been Your Life.*' Possible cultural references: *Back to the Future* (film); *Heroes* (TV); film and music personalities who died 'prematurely' (Heath Ledger; Kurt Cobain).

3   *Make impersonal observations of how specific religious principles determine responses to particular issues.* Discussion: Would it have been bad if human beings had never existed? Link to Christian approaches ('God is Love'), Judaic (Covenant with Abraham) and or Islamic notions of humans ability to appreciate 'God's work' (the essential goodness of creation). Contrast with the non-theistic Buddhism's attempts to realize the purpose of creation through resisting self-regard.

Enrichment: Distinguish between natural theology – what can be known about God from consideration about the created world in general (see Thomas Aquinas' *teleological argument*) and a 'theology of nature' – what a religious tradition and historical revelations say about the natural world.

Further reading and resources

Eiseley, L. (1973) *The Immense Journey.* New York: Vintage Books.

The author, who is an anthropologist and naturalist, 'contemplates the mysteries of nature' through a review of his experiences.

Fortey, R. (1997) *Life: An Unauthorized Biography.* New York: HarperCollins.

An exploration of the natural history of the first four thousand million years of life on and in the Earth.

Sagan, C. (1996) *Pale Blue Dot: A Vision of the Human Future in Space.* New York: Random House.

This book examines 'humankind's changing awareness of its place in the universe and the rich potential of human ventures into the world beyond Earth'.

Ward, K. (1996) *Religion & Creation*. Oxford: Clarendon Press.

This book explores the idea of a creator God in the work of twentieth-century writers from Judaism, Islam, Hinduism, and Christianity. It also presents a Trinitarian doctrine of creation, drawing inspiration from a wider set of theistic traditions and recent discussions in physics in the realm of cosmology.

Lesson 2: The importance of being me

This lesson focuses on the individual; the nature of personal identity, the notion of a spiritual dimension to the self, its relationship to our physical body and associated religious explanations.

The lesson begins with an exploration of the life-histories of 'well-known' individuals to gain an appreciation of how a person's attributes (physical, cultural, moral, ethical, spiritual, personal etc.) might appear to remain constant but change – perhaps intentionally – over time. The lesson then continues with an analysis of the range and types of attributes your students posses; their commonalities and differences, which will give your students a personal basis for their examination how different religions makes sense of how the individual self is 'linked' to others, the divine and religious notions of human 'purpose'. Inclusion of the materialist's perspective on human life will also provoke issues and questions that will be explored in greater detail in the next lesson.

Key words and phrases

Anatta (no-self), anicca (impermanence), identity, materialism, mind-body, no-self, purpose, rebirth, self, selfishness, soul, spirit.

Key learning objectives

By the end of the lesson all will:

* know that we all form notions of ourselves containing elements that are relatively stable throughout our lives, whilst others are open to profound changes, which may be emotional or spiritual in character.

By the end of the lesson most will:

- reflect on questions that examine the extent to which a purposeful human existence requires the necessity of a creator God.

By the end of the lesson some will:

- understand how different religious traditions attempt to understand the relationship between the material body and the non-materialistic 'spirit'.

Concepts

From a religious tradition:

- consider the possible meaning of *anatta* (no-self) and the possibility of their being a non-personal understanding of transcendence.

From human experience:

- reflect on what constitutes our sense of ourselves and others.

From the study of religion:

- investigate the notion of an embodied spirit and the importance of an individual.

Background briefing

Our ability to think about ourselves as individuals comes into being during the course of our early interactions with others. Initially, we begin by realising that we have a *point* of view and that one is a being with all sorts of attributes. The individual develops their view based on the views of more skilled performers (family members, friends and teachers), with further developments occurring when we take over and undertake this process for ourselves – by supplementing our learning from others – and becoming a *point* of action (the 'I' that does things; expressed in the use of first- and second-person pronouns and grammatically similar constructions). Now we are able to complete tasks for ourselves, from which arises a sense of personal responsibility.

Practices characteristic of one's culture shape and modulate our developing sense of identity. Persons and events with which we have a sense of belonging are ways in which any religious or cultural influences are integrated into an individual's self – becoming the way the we develop a more multi-faceted self – allowing one to incorporate distinctions appropriated from a wider range of sources, not just our personal experiences, but also from traditional, cultural, or collective memories, narratives and texts.

To have a sense of self you need; a 'multi-vocal' sense of one's location as a person:

1   the point of view from which one perceives the material environment and acts on it – unique to the individual's spatial location – a singularity – a sense of personal *distinctness*
2   the totality of personal attributes – includes our more or less stable physical make-up and the highly changeable patterns of thoughts and actions
3   the totalities of personal impressions we make on other people.

These multiple narratives we have of ourselves nevertheless express the sense one has of one's life as a unity in time, tied together by the use of 'I' – every 'telling' reflects our beliefs about point 2, expressed, very often to others as point 3 – is woven together into an embodied person. We tell *situated stories* – narrative accounts of personal memory that have been created within a specific situation, by particular individuals, for particular audiences, and to fulfil particular goals – to develop and maintain the self.

There are many ways that individuals' notions of themselves can be influenced by religious or cultural ideas. Some societies pressure individuals to conform to standard values and behaviour patterns, whereas others permit a broad range of diversity and deviance. Some societies embed the self in a complex web of multiple relationships so that a single person performs many different roles, while others keep each individual in one or two well-defined groups, which he or she can ill afford to alienate. Some societies place paramount value on sincerity and authenticity, which means that the person is expected to be true to his or her inner convictions, but in other societies the important thing is that publicly visible behaviour be proper and appropriate to prevailing norms, regardless of what beliefs that person may privately entertain.

Lesson structure

1 Opener: Teacher to bring in photographs of themselves (or another, perhaps 'well known' adult) which show them in various 'life-stages'. Show students the images and talk about what changes might take place in the way a person views themselves, their position in the world, their beliefs and values, their relationship with others and spiritual/religious matters.

2 *Use their personal experiences to engage with specific issues.* Ask each student to undertake a similar task using a photograph of themselves (previously asked to be brought in). Are they the same person now as they were in the picture? What has changed and what has remained the same? Will they be the same person in five or ten years time?

   Plenary: Do individual students change in general ways? Highlight specific and general issues that are raised. For example: notions of identity and self. Working criteria for what constitutes an individual. Possible contemporary cultural links: personal identities portrayed on Facebook or other social-networking sites; the use of avatars and aliases in gaming scenarios. Use role-play and paired discussions to highlight alternate perspectives.

   Make impersonal observations of how specific religious principles determine responses to particular issues. Introduce Buddhism's five *skandhas* – the five constituent elements that make up a person – namely: physical form, feelings, perceptions, volitions and consciousness, and the concept of *anicca* (impermanence). Contrast these with Abrahamic faith assumptions that there exists a substantial, eternal self or *spirit*. Contrast both of the above with a natural materialist account that an individual life has essentially no purpose other that what we endow it with, and the opportunity to pass on one's genetic heritage.

   Examine Hindu and Buddhist notions of *deva*, how the Buddha attained *nibbana*, and how followers might also reach this goal through 'rebirth' and *anatta* 'no-self'.

3 *Enable students to reflect on their emotional response to issues.* Discussion: Does a person's life serve any purpose? How does Buddhism make you feel about how people should view themselves, the 'importance' of who they are and the actions they undertake? Where should we take meaning and purpose from if not from our 'salvation', 'atonement' of our sins or place in the 'afterlife'? Would a purely materialist account focusing on aesthetics and pleasure be a more realistic position?

Enrichment: Explore more fully the difficulties and issues surrounding the notion of an embodied soul and the notion of 'spirit' in different religious traditions; Buddhist means towards reducing a sense of self and attachment through meditation.

Further reading and resources

Harré, R. (1998) *The Singular Self.* London: Sage.

Drawing on material from psychology, philosophy, anthropology and linguistics, this books aims to develop a scientific account of personhood.

Humphrey, N. (2002) *The Mind Made Flesh.* Oxford: Oxford University Press.

This collection includes essays on: the evolution of consciousness, the nature of the self, multiple personality disorder, cave art and religious miracles.

Ward, K. (1998) *Religion & Human Nature.* Oxford: Clarendon Press.

This book deals with religious views of human nature and destiny. The beliefs of six major traditions are presented. The impact of scientific theories about the cosmic and biological evolution of religious beliefs is assessed, and a form of 'soft emergent materialism' is defended, with regard to the soul.

'Darwin and Humanity: Should we Rid the Mind of God?' (2007).

A special debate between Alister McGrath, author of *The Dawkins Delusion* and Peter Atkins, well known atheist and author [www.atheistdebate.org].

Lesson 3: Death: disintegration or destiny?

This lesson leads on from issues explored in the previous lesson and focuses on our collective memories and the impact that human beings can have on the ideas, customs and actions of others.

The lesson initially looks at the aims and objectives of funeral rights in different cultures, and then investigates the religious principles underpinning the symbols and practices involved with memorials for the departed and their importance to the living. Focusing on funereal practices – both religious and non-religious – the lesson enables students to explore both their personal and objective responses to the legacy of individuals, and makes links to the issues surrounding our notions of physicalism, which is more fully examined in the next lesson.

Key words and phrases

Death, memorials, memory, rebirth, remembrance.

Key learning objectives

By the end of the lesson all will:

- know that the rituals and customs surrounding death, funerals and remembrance of the departed, play a significant role in all cultures: both ancient and modern.

By the end of the lesson most will:

- reflect on how different attitudes to death alter the way individuals deal with death and acknowledge the departed.

By the end of the lesson some will:

- understand how death and the departed are integral to most religious traditions and the lives of their adherents.

Concepts

From a religious tradition:

- suggests how a person's actions during their life affects what happens on their death.

From human experience:

- reflect on the importance of being remembered and remembering others.

From the study of religion:

- investigate the role of death, memory and memorials in the lives of the living.

Background briefing

Our memories and our views of ourselves are interconnected, forming a database of the self, with every individual *actively* and *constantly* reshaping their use of autobiographical knowledge. How we construct our view of ourselves appears to be dependent upon our cultural upbringing, reflected in the different ways our memories are remembered, described and used.

Some individuals will make use of elaborate and detailed memories of autobiographical events that focus on their own roles, preferences, and feelings. Whereas others, brought up and living within a distinctly different cultural heritage, will tend to focus on past experiences that centre on communal descriptions of themselves in terms of their interdependent, social roles.

The skill of manipulating autobiographical knowledge appears to develop gradually, *emerging* over time: as we begin to make use of our knowledge of our own past experiences and actions, to develop an his-torical context – through talk with others – to our autobiographical memories. In this way we are able to develop self-narratives that are *personally meaningful*. This is especially salient during adolescence, where the individual's need to make sense of where they 'fit in' to their familial and societal structures often becomes a consuming issue, as they grapple with their new-found ability for introspection.

Thus, developing a coherent, narrative 'me' provides us with a successful working model for organizing our own personal memories, whilst at the same time allowing us to learn and practice the use of forms of behaviour valued and recognized by the community in which we live.

Lesson structure

1 *Make impersonal observations of how specific religious principles determine responses to particular issues.* Opener: Do funerals have to be solemn occasions? Recount the Mexican festival, the Day of the Dead; a New Orleans jazz funeral; Chinese Confucian graveyard picnics or similar events.

2 What is the significance of different funeral colours worn by different cultures: black, white, red and black? How have lights been used as metaphors and symbols for lives (votive candles; Jewish memorial lights and Shoah black candles; Japanese paper lanterns)? How do different religious traditions accommodate death and the dead: the importance of ancestors and remembering the departed?

3 *Enable students to reflect on their emotional response to issues.* Use examples of burial services and mourners' rituals (including humanist funerals – www.humanism.org.uk) to illustrate similarities and differences.

4 *Use their personal experiences to engage with specific issues.* In small, private groups, ask students to recall their own responses to attending a funeral. Alternately (and less personally significant) watch the public outpouring of grief, and the reaction to the death of a public figure, such as Diana, Princess of Wales, or public responses to national days of remembrance ('Poppy' Day; Holocaust Memorial Day). Would they ever respond the

same way? What makes people show, or inhibits them from displaying, public sorrow or affection for the loss of others?

Enrichment: Look at memorials and monuments to the dead: memorials (e.g. Yad Vashem: www.yadvashem.org or the Taj Mahal); tombs (e.g. Terracotta Army); pyramids; long barrows; sculptures; epics poems; songs and eulogies. What do they tell us about the religious and cultural attitudes to death in ancient and contemporary cultures?

Further reading and resources

Chown, M. (2007) *The Never-ending Days of Being Dead*. London: Faber & Faber.

This book looks at 'the nature of reality and the place of life in the universe'.

Dennett, D. C. (1995) *Darwin's Dangerous Idea: Evolution and the Meanings of Life*. New York: Simon & Schuster.

This book assesses Darwin's theory of evolution and looks at why it gives rise to such heated debate among scientists, philosophers and sociologists. The book aims to 'show that Darwinism does not devalue the miracles of life'.

Sullivan, L. E. (1989) *Death, Afterlife and the Soul*. New York: Macmillan Press.

This book explores the traditions and rites of death, the varying perception of the afterlife, the transition to the underworld and the differing conceptions of the soul and destiny.

Lesson 4: From dust, to dust once again

This lesson explores the role of the physical body to a person's sense of identity. Students are initially asked to focus on inanimate objects, the 'conservation' of the matter of which all things are composed, and then expand their appreciation to include animate objects.

Examination of materialist and religious explanations of cycles then allows students to make sense of alternative funeral rites, their differing emphases on the importance of preserving the physical body and how this encapsulates a particular religion's understanding of how they might connect the material and spiritual realms.

Key words and phrases

Animism, conservation of matter, cycles, impermanence, permanence, personhood, physicalism.

Key learning objectives

By the end of the lesson all will:

- know that, for many people with a religious belief, a person is more than its physical body.

By the end of the lesson most will:

- reflect on the ways in which scientific and religious world views, such as Hinduism, understand material origins in terms of cyclical processes.

By the end of the lesson some will:

- understand how different religious traditions attempt to relate the animate and inanimate.

Concepts

From a religious tradition:

- suggest how the material and the non-material (spiritual) can be understood in terms of a cosmological understanding of their origins.

From human experience:

- appreciate the tensions generated between our understanding of material permanence and the impermanence of individual human beings.

From the study of religion:

- reflect on the relative importance of the physical body and the notion of the 'person'.

Background briefing

One author who contemplated the ambiguous relationships people have with the physical world – the fragility and impermanence of human lives, the role our bodies play in shaping our identities and the way our bodies can endure suffering, pain and deprivation – was Primo Levi.

Levi was born, and lived for most of his life, in Turin, Italy until his death in 1987. Before the Second World War he trained and worked as an industrial chemist. It was his profession that saved his life, as he was interred and assigned to an industrial unit by the Nazis rather than sent for extermination at Auschwitz. These experiences have been famously recorded in his autobiographical works, *If This is a Man, The Truce* and *The*

Drowned and the Saved.

In his book *The Periodic Table*, published in 1978, each of the 21 chapters (or elements) analyses different facets of the human condition and are used as *aides-memoires* for his own autobiographical reflections on his life from his beginnings as an amateur chemist through to his subsequent capture, internment in, and post-war journey from, Auschwitz and beyond. The book's final chapter, 'Carbon', is Levi's conscious attempt to show that scientific processes are as much a part of the reader's makeup as they are his own.

Levi realized that people tended not to appreciate the vitality of physical processes. Static, textbook accounts of chemical reactions make it difficult for anyone to envisage the dynamic energy that permeates all change. For a more realistic understanding, what was required was an appreciation of the processes underlying material changes as well as the reagents involved or the products made.

Levi's Carbon Cycle describes the places and processes by which the element carbon moves around the Earth. Carbon can be found in the land, water and air in many different forms, as it combines with other elements to form compounds. It is a cycle, because the total amount of carbon remains the same — it is just recycled and found in a different place. The greenhouse effect, for example, is of concern because a higher percentage of carbon is in the atmosphere than is usually the case and this is affecting the Earth's climate.

An additional reason why the carbon cycle is important to appreciate and understand is that, as part of the recycling of carbon, it describes how all living things (including humans) obtain their food, grow, live, breathe and die and how this is integrated into a wider picture of how the Earth works.

Levi's 'epic' account of the carbon cycle is a depiction of the 'journey' of a single carbon atom; from limestone cliff, through the air and oceans, to its incorporation into the grapes on a vine and, ultimately, finding itself in a glass of wine drunk by the author. It's final 'use', before being, once again, exhaled, is to 'help' Levi in the process of transmitting his ideas by bringing together the writer and reader in a single instant, as his hand makes, and our eyes read, the final full stop of the chapter.

Lesson structure

1 Opener: Hold up an everyday object (e.g. a plant, candle or rock) and tell the story of its 'life': its origins, the processes it has had to endure, the possible 'futures' for the matter it contains.

   Use their personal experiences to engage with specific issues. Explore with students the scientific notion of 'conservation of matter'. Let students draw, write or dramatize a 'life story' (cf. Levi's 'Carbon') of their own choosing.

2 *Make impersonal observations of how specific religious principles determine responses to particular issues.* Examine pictures or, preferably, an actual *Nataraj* (http://www.sanatansociety.org/hindu_gods_and_goddesses/shiva.htm). Explain its various component elements and overall symbolic meaning and its place in a Hindu cosmological understanding – especially the concept of *yugas* (age cycles).

   Discussion: Compare and contrast this with 'scientific' cycles: such as material cycles explaining the birth, death and destruction of stars, water recycling, or the recycling of rubbish. Are there similarities? How are both science and spirituality accommodated into the Hindu world view? (see http://www.hinduism.co.za/)

3 *Enable students to reflect on their emotional response to issues.* Plenary: Recall appropriate phrases from the humanist (and one other) funeral ceremonies examined in the previous lesson. Explore with students the importance of the preservation of physical remains in Judaism, Islam or for a Jehovah's Witness, and contrast that with religious traditions than require cremation (Shintoism, Hinduism and Buddhism).

   Discussion: What is their understanding of the term 'person' or 'personhood'? Do you stop being a person once you die? Is their body important to them? Why and what is its purpose?

   Alternate debate: Would they like their body to be preserved and why (http://www.cryonics.org/)? Are student responses similar to the conjectured reasons as to why Aztecs or ancient Egyptians 'mummified' their dead?

   Enrichment: Explore animistic religious traditional notions (such as West African or Australian Aboriginal) of the spiritual connections between the animate and inanimate worlds.

Further reading and resources

Atkins, P. (1992) *Creation Revisited*. London: Penguin.

This book explores 'the fundamental questions of modern science: the existence of the universe, time, chance, life and consciousness'.

Chown, M. (2000) *The Magic Furnace*. London: Vintage.

This book is an historical account of how astronomers and nuclear physicists deduced where the elements in our bodies come from.

Faraday, M. (1871/2007) *The Chemical History of a Candle*. London: Standard Publications.

An unabridged version of the six lectures Faraday delivered to young students at London's Royal Institution in 1860–61.

Levi, P. (1985) 'Carbon' in *The Periodic Table*, trans. Raymond Rosenthal. London: Michael Joseph.

Lesson 5: Am I 'special' or not?

This lesson asks your students to look at a range of unfamiliar and familiar creation myths and stories to identify similarities and differences in the ways they describe the process of creation and the relationship between Creator and their Creation.

Students then go on to explore the reasons why creation accounts are found in religious texts and the ways these have been read to make sense of human beings' 'place' and 'purpose'. The lesson also gives students the opportunity to draw on information addressed in the previous lessons as they formulate issues and questions that require further scrutiny in the final session.

Key words and phrases

Creation, human existence, myths, purpose, rationale, stories.

Key learning objectives

By the end of the lesson all will:

*   know that, for many people, creation narratives are necessary in order to give meaning and purpose to human existence.

By the end of the lesson most will:

*   reflect on the linguistic and stylistic differences between religious and non-religious narratives, and how this has influenced how they are interpreted.

By the end of the lesson some will:

*   suggest what explanations may be given to understand a Creator's purpose for their Creation.

Concepts

From a religious tradition:

- suggest how scriptural writings may be read and understood to perceive the role of human beings in Creation.

From human experience:

- reflect on how creation narratives are used to explain human origin and purpose.

From the study of religion:

- identify the various different ways of defining the terms: Creator and Creation.

Lesson structure

1 Opener: Perform a dramatized account of a creation story which would be unfamiliar to your students, given their cultural backgrounds.
2 *Enable students to reflect on their emotional response to issues.* Ask students to perform or read through a range of other creation stories (Celtic, Native American, ancient Greek, Confucian, Icelandic) recounting the origin of human beings.
3 *Use their personal experiences to engage with specific issues.* Discussion: According to the creation myths, were humans 'created' in ways that were different or special from other animals? With which divine characteristics were humans imbued by their Creators?

    Contrast these with stories of origins drawn from science fiction/ fantasy books or films. Do these 'fictional' accounts deal with similar issues (purpose of the Created, rationale for existence, needs of the Creator) to those found in the creations myths?

    Make impersonal observations of how specific religious principles determine responses to particular issues. Compare and contrast scriptural accounts of human creation. What are the specific and general issues that can be drawn from these verses?

Plenary: What are the purposes (human and divine) for the inclusion of creation accounts in religious holy books? Should they be 'read' in the same way as scientific literature?

Enrichment: Look at the Abrahamic faiths' linguistic and symbolic uses of inanimate objects, (rock, dust, sand, specks etc.), as comparators to the living imbued with 'the breath of God' or the 'spark of life'.

Examine the strengths and weaknesses of some religious believers and process theologians' arguments regarding God's 'need' to produce loving Creations. What does this imply about God, his Creations and their ability to make 'free choices'?

Further reading and resources

Smolin, L. (1997) *Life in the Cosmos*. Oxford: Weidenfeld & Nicholson.
   This book puts forward a view of the cosmos that 'moves beyond both the notion of God and the pessimism of Nietzsche and the existentialists'.

Science and Religion in Schools Project (2006) *Science and Religion in Schools*. Victoria, BC: Trafford Publishing. Topic 4b: What do religions say about the beginning of the universe?

Ward, K. (1996) *Religion & Creation*. Oxford: Clarendon Press.

Lesson 6: So what is the truth and how do I decide?

This lesson has as its focus on one of the main themes that is central to the study of religion namely, the nature of truth. We have already examined in Chapter 5 some of the differences between truth claims in religion and science. This lesson aims to enable your students to make use of such distinctions when examining scriptural accounts and understand the different ways religious texts are used by their adherents.

Key words and phrases

Context, detail, emergence, explanation, interpretation, perspective, truth.

Key learning objectives

By the end of the lesson all will:

- know that people use the term 'true' in different ways.

By the end of the lesson most will:

- know that the explanatory power of information is dependent on the question asked.

By the end of the lesson some will:

- reflect on their own and others' questions about truth.

Concepts

From a religious tradition:

- suggest that religious truths may also emerge from the interpretation of scriptural accounts.

From human experience:

- reflect on the our need to seek truth and meaning from explanations and events.

From the study of religion:

- investigate how scriptural accounts can be used to assert truth claims.

Lesson structure

1 Opener: 'What makes something 'true'? Ask students to make a 'true likeness' drawing of an object (car, fruit, jug). Were they able to 'capture' the shadows, textures effectively? Would a photograph be any better? What about all the non-visual aspects (sound of the engine's power; smell of the ripe fruit) that's missing? Would more detail necessarily give a better understanding (see *Powers of 10*, http://powersof10.com/ or Google Earth)?

2 *Make impersonal observations of how specific religious principles determine responses to particular issues.* Look at a range of different styles of portraiture (cartoon, courtroom sketch, formal portraits of monarchs, advertising shots). What truths are they trying to capture and portray? How successful are they? What additional information (contemporary, cultural, political and geographical knowledge, symbolic use of posture and objects, contemporary and idiomatic pictorial vocabulary) did you require to be able to make sense of the images? Were some of the images easier to 'decode' than others?

Now look at a range of religious images, for example: Orthodox Christian icons, Hindu deities, Islamic calligraphy, the Passover *Haggadah* or statues of Buddha. In what ways can these be 'read' by the religious adherent?

3   *Use their personal experiences to engage with specific issues.* Look at a number of Gospel accounts that describe the same part of Jesus' life (e.g. his Resurrection, the Last Supper). Are their descriptions consistent? Which one is true: one, none or all? Where does the truth reside, in the accuracy of the gospel writers' accounts, our interpretation of their writings or an *emerging* understanding of an event seen from a range of perspectives?

Discussion: Are truths only to be found within the account of Jesus' life: religious or historical? Are not religious truths also 'revealed' when trying to understand the parables, for example?

4   *Enable students to reflect on their emotional response to issues.* Explanations and the questions they answer: Look at Edwin A. Abbott's (1994) *Flatland: A Parable of Spiritual Dimensions.* Oxford: Oneworld. Here is an example of a 'parable' that explores our ability to understand and explain the events that occur, and the opportunity for 'truth' to be missed and then revealed by our inability to perceive events from more than one perspective.

Plenary: What guides us to making sense of our world, our actions and ourselves? What is the most appropriate place to seek understanding to explain a particular issue? Can religion or science explain everything to our satisfaction?

Further reading and resources

Chandrasekhar, S. (1987) *Truth and Beauty: Aesthetics and Motivations in Science.* Chicago: University of Chicago Press.

Science and Religion in Schools Project (2006) *Science and Religion in Schools.* Victoria, BC: Trafford Publishing. Topic 2a: What is an explanation?

Weinberg, S. (1993) *Dreams of a Final Theory: Search for the Ultimate Laws of Nature.* New York: Hutchinson.

This book is a defence of reductionism (the impulse to trace explanations of natural phenomena to deeper and deeper levels), and 'examines the curious relevance of beauty and symmetry in scientific theories'.

Wolpert, L. (2000) *The Unnatural Nature of Science*. London: Faber and Faber.

This book aims to show that many of our understandings about scientific thought can be corrected once we realize just how 'unnatural' science actually is.

Further reading

Appleyard, B. (2004) *Understanding the Present: An Alternative History of Science*. London: Tauris Parke.

This book describes the progression of scientific knowledge, from Copernicus and Descartes to Einstein and Hawking, and 'its devastating impact on mankind's belief in his dominant role in the universe'.

Dawkins, R. (1998) *Unweaving the Rainbow*. London: Allen Lane.

Keats accused Newton of destroying the poetry of the rainbow by explaining the origin of its colours. This book argues that Keats could not have been more mistaken, and shows how an understanding of science 'enhances our wonder of the world'.

Qualifications and Curriculum Authority (2007) *Religious Education Programme of Study (Non-statutory) for Key Stage 3*. London: QCA.

Sagan, C. (1996) *The Demon-Haunted World: Science as a Candle in the Dark*. New York: Headline.

This book reflects on the current state of scientific thought and aims to refute the arguments that science destroys spirituality.

Scottish Government (2009) *Curriculum for Excellence: Religious and Moral Education*. Edinburgh: Learning & Teaching Scotland.

Thomas, L. (1983) *Late Night Thoughts on Listening to Mahler's 'Ninth Symphony'*. New York: Viking Penguin.

Welsh Assembly Government (2008) *National Exemplar Framework for Religious Education for 3 to 19-year-olds in Wales: Guidance for Local Education Authorities and Agreed Syllabus Conferences*. Cardiff: Curriculum and Assessment Division.

Chapter 8

Planning lessons for ages 16–19

Chapter overview

This chapter explores how lessons using our pedagogical approach might be planned and taught to students in the upper-secondary age phase (16–19). Teaching objectives are, primarily, taken from England's National Curriculum for religious education, – although additional material has been drawn from the Wales' National Exemplar Framework, and Scotland's *Curriculum for Excellence* – with exemplar lesson plans then showing how the learning objectives could be addressed and how religion and science topics could be used to explore wider religious education concepts. Throughout the chapter, background briefings are included to give a context to the scientific ideas being explored.

What do teachers need to know?

What are the essential skills and processes in religious education that a student needs to learn to make progress? When *learning about religion* at this level, students should be able to:

- investigate and interpret significant issues in relation to the impact of religious beliefs and teachings on individuals, communities and societies

- use and develop their specialist religious and philosophical vocabulary, recognizing both its power and limitations in expressing religious ideas and beliefs.

When *learning from religion* at this level, students should be able to:

- reflect critically on their opinions in the light of their learning about the relationship between beliefs, teachings, world issues and ultimate questions
- develop their independent values and attitudes on moral and spiritual issues related to their autonomy, identities, rights and responsibilities
- evaluate issues, beliefs, commitments and the influence of religion, including philosophical, spiritual and ethical perspectives.

Engagement with religion and science topics, as explored in the exemplar lesson plans below, will enable your students to address all of the above points. As we stated previously, religion and science topics are best explored not in isolation but integrated into your religious education planning as a means of examining the key concepts and principles of religious education. The learning objectives of the exemplar lessons are, therefore, merely illustrative of the pedagogic approach promoted in this book. They are not intended to be 'off the peg' teaching units, but could easily be adapted and extended to fit your particular curriculum planning requirements.

Description of the exemplar lessons

The six lessons explore some of the main religious and philosophical questions surrounding the role and purpose of the physical body, our knowledge of our origins, human suffering, individual and collective responsibility and human agency. The final lesson draws on the learning that has taken place in the previous lessons, as it examines the meanings and purposes given to human life in scriptural and theological writings and teachings.

What do students need to know?

Your students will need to be able to analyse teachings, sources, authorities and ways of life in order to understand religions and beliefs, as they examine systems of thought that are religious and non-religious, theistic and non-theistic, Western and Eastern, Abrahamic and dharmic. They will also need to understand how religious practices can help individuals and communities give expression to their questions and answers in various ways, the impact such assumptions may have and the way they may underpin decisions and lifestyles.

Students will then be able to interpret and evaluate many different sources and forms of religious, spiritual, moral and cultural expression, which will enable them to analyse and synthesize their insights on some of the ethical, spiritual or philosophical questions that confront humanity. They will also be in a position to evaluate their own and others' values, to understand reasons for a belief or commitment they do not share, and empathize with the experiences of those with whom they do not agree. They should also be able to acknowledge the strengths and weaknesses of their own beliefs, and see their attitudes, values and behaviour as others see them.

Lesson 1: In praise of perfection

In this first lesson we focus on the human body: its appearance and fragility and its ability – or lack of – to 'project' an accurate depiction of ourselves, who we are and what we (and, perhaps, God) might like us to be.

Because of the potentially sensitive nature of the subject matter being discussed, the 'ground rules' discussed in Chapter 6 might be usefully employed as way of allowing all your students to feel comfortable and able to participate in all the activities.

Key words and phrases

Body, modesty, perfection, salvation, soul.

Key learning objectives

By the end of the lesson all will:

- know that for the followers of the Abrahamic faiths, in particular, individual salvation has been most often (but not exclusively) associated with a focus on the purely spiritual.

By the end of the lesson most will:

- reflect on the reasons underlying the apparent tensions between contemporary importance on physical appearance and religious strictures.

By the end of the lesson some will:

- suggest how, historically, our understanding of being made in God's image has changed.

Concepts

From a religious tradition:

- suggest how the physical body is often seen as an impediment to spiritual development.

From human experience:

- reflect on how the pursuit of perfection and the removal of disability are seen as positive.

From the study of religion:

- identify how different theological thinkers have interpreted the notion that human beings are made in God's likeness.

Background briefing

This first lesson allows your students to focus on the importance of the individual: its importance to the way they view their understanding of religions, related theological approaches and possible, alternate philosophical perspectives.

We start with personal reactions to the importance of the physical body and then focus on religious responses to its relevance, or otherwise, to personal, spiritual development.

Lesson structure

1 *Enable students to reflect on their emotional response to issues.* Opener: Give each student a small hand-held mirror. Ask them to study their own face and list five aspects that they think they are happy with, and any that could be improved. Give them sets of magazines – ask them to compile a collage of their 'perfect' male/female face.

Use their personal experiences to engage with specific issues. Discussion: What makes a perfect face (symmetry, lack of blemishes, skin colour)? Why are beauty treatments (cosmetic surgery), dieting and self-image important to many (especially young people)? Examine the Islamic notion of modesty.

If we are all made in God's image, should we be trying to improve on/alter that image? Should physical impairment, such as deafness, be viewed as a disability?

2 *Make impersonal observations of how specific religious principles determine responses to particular issues.* Explore in greater detail some of the theological interpretations (Christian, Judaic and Islamic) of the notion that human beings are made in God's likeness. Examine how early Christian thought accommodated classical Greek (see Aristotle's *De Anima* and Plato's *Ideals*) ideas of perfection and the form of the body. How later thinkers (esp. Aquinas', *Summa Theologiae*) reduced the importance of the physical body – to the physical receptacle of the soul at the Last Judgement – with an ever-increasing emphasis on spiritual salvation.

Discussion: Does an ever-increasing knowledge of our body and our technological ability to 'improve' and enhance it, diminish or increase its importance? Have people become too focused on the body?

Enrichment: Examine the use of physical deprivation in religious pursuits (such as fasting, pilgrimage or seclusion – retreats, hermits, monasteries) as means towards spiritual development. Contrast this with the physical focus on dieting, exercise, 'detox' and the development of institutions such as the health farm and occupations such as personal trainers.

Mirror the focus on Christian attitudes to the body with the study of ascetic approaches of other religious traditions.

Contrast with religious views about how important it is for the body to be healthy (e.g. yoga)? For example, Buddhists are much more behaviourist in that our consciousness/mind cannot be healthy spiritually unless it is mindful, so successful meditation requires physical dedication as well!

Further reading and resources

Gilman, S. L. (2000) *Making the Body Beautiful: A Cultural History of Aesthetic Surgery*. Princeton: Princeton University Press.

This book argues that aesthetic surgery has such universal appeal because it helps people to 'pass' and to be seen as a member of a group with which they want to or need to identify.

Sacks, O. (1986) *The Man Who Mistook His Wife for a Hat*. London: Picador.

This book looks at what happens when things go wrong with parts of the brain and how our behaviour is altered.

Science and Religion in Schools Project (2006) *Science and Religion in Schools*. Victoria, BC: Trafford Publishing. Topic 6b: Medical Ethics and Biotechnology.

Ward, K. (1998) *Religion & Human Nature*. Oxford: Clarendon Press.

Lesson 2: How did we get to here?

This lesson is an attempt to stop your students simply compartmentalizing their scientific and religious understandings of the world, by exploring the limitations and implications of the Darwinian evolutionary model.

Initially, students are first asked to role-play some of the contemporary Victorian reactions to Darwin's evolutionary theory to elicit a variety of perspectives without advocating one particular view. Such an historical exploration of the interaction between Darwin's religious and scientific world views will help your students to gain an appreciation of an individual scientist's response to cultural, social and personal influences on their work such as, for example, how Darwin came to terms with the early death of his daughter Annie. The skills developed in such an historical analysis can then be employed when students go on to explore contemporary developments in evolutionary theory and theological reactions to modern scientific developments.

Key words and phrases

Anthropic principle, emergence, evolution, fitness, heritability, transcendence, variation.

Key learning objectives

By the end of the lesson all will:

- know the main bases of Darwin's evolutionary theory.

By the end of the lesson most will:

- reflect on how Darwin's evolutionary theory caused theological interpretations of human origins to be reassessed.

By the end of the lesson some will:

- suggest what are the main points of dissent from contemporary evolutionary approaches for particular groups of religious adherents.

Concepts

From a religious tradition:

- suggest how human beings' relationship to God has been reinterpreted in the light of scientific developments.

From human experience:

- reflect on how an appreciation of the history of development in evolutionary theory has altered the way biological systems are perceived.

From the study of religion:

- identify the different ways religious adherents respond to science's evolutionary explanations of human origins.

Background briefing

What emerges from the historical research into the interaction between Darwin's religious and scientific world views is a picture of an individual in whom scientific and religious questions developed a reciprocal relationship as he moved more or less steadily from almost total orthodoxy in his youth, to complete agnosticism in the years after the *Origin*, to the ambivalent state that particularly characterized him in the final phase of his life; one of intermittent and largely agnostic theism.

Darwin was, therefore, a person who was simultaneously trying to understand his own religious sentiments – and by inference those of others – whilst searching for a naturalistic understanding of what it is to be human. Therefore Darwin should be seen as a person with a view of the world informed, and which can only be made sense of by the interweaving of his science and personal beliefs.

In fact, the evident appreciation shown by Darwin of how theistic arguments might influence a person's understanding of his evolutionary theory is indicative of a general approach seen in his writings, in which Darwin appears to be trying to reconcile his personal moral or religious values with his developing scientific understanding of the world. Indeed, it would appear that at the time of writing the *Origin* Darwin is still wishing to persuade his readers that their notion of God was religiously, rather than scientifically, limited.

For Darwin the origins of religions were a natural evolutionary progression as, he wrote in *The Descent of Man*, man would have 'craved to understand what was passing around him, and have vaguely speculated on his own existence' (p. 65). Thus, it is not surprising that he invested his methodological approach with an unambiguously moral content, and so it should come as little surprise then that in *Descent* we find Darwin addressing the 'great sin of slavery' in the same paragraph that he confronts the 'horrible cruelty to animals' (p. 94).

It must be stressed that Darwin was not sympathetic to conventional religious objectives. Nor should Darwin ever be thought of as a naturalist for whom theology might have a positive bearing on science. Nevertheless, Darwin's evolutionary project was the best means by which Darwin could make sense of the world in which he lived; not just in terms of his scientific ideas, his moral reaction to slavery and religious variation in diverse civilisations, but also his hopes for the future – a philosophy of Nature and Man appropriate for an industrial age.

This can be seen by the fact that when Darwin formed and expressed his ideas of progress in the fullest sense he drew on non-scientific sources, including theology. Therefore, his work could be seen as the autonomous discernment of natural laws, whilst acknowledging the possibility of God's existence as the 'first' cause for an awesome – though largely inscrutable – design that was eventually realized in the evolution of conscious selves.

Lesson structure

1 *Use their personal experiences to engage with specific issues.* Opener: How did we get here? After 'setting the scene' and supplying background context and briefing materials, ask students to role-play some of the contemporary Victorian reactions to Darwin's evolutionary theory (you may wish to use artistic 're-imaginings', such as the 2009 film *Creation*). What arguments might Darwin's supporters use to 'win over' their proponents? What counter-arguments could be deployed? Do any of the issues discussed remain pertinent today?

2 *Make impersonal observations of how specific religious principles determine responses to particular issues.* How can religious accounts of human origins be reconciled with a scientific, evolutionary understanding? Examine evolutionary theorists before Darwin (Paley's *Natural Theology*, Lamarck's 'transmutation') and how Darwin's *Origin* was a significant change in biological understanding based on the three intertwining concepts of *variation*, *heritability* and *fitness*.

   What were the main challenges of Darwin's theory to nineteenth-century theology (that creation is not individually designed *directly* by God, but builds upon science's understanding of the Earth's age and its geological development as proposed by Lyell. It also implies that apes and humans share a common ancestor – as described in *The Descent of Man*)?

   Enable students to reflect on their emotional response to issues. How has contemporary knowledge of genetic inheritance led to the emergence of strong materialistic reductionism (such as the works of Francis Crick, Richard Dawkins and E. O. Wilson), which purport that *all* biological systems will ultimately be explained in terms of physics and chemistry (see www.richarddawkins.net)?

   Discussion: If a person accepts Darwin's theory, how can the idea of God be accommodated into their way of thinking?

In reviewing how the above question may be answered, also introduce some of the non-materialistic responses. These could include:
questioning the authority of evolutionary theory; the 'repositioning'
of theology to a more 'naturalistic' relationship between human beings
and nature (see Teilhard de Chardin's *The Phenomenon of Man*). You may
also wish to outline arguments that appear to suggest the necessity of a
Creator to explain the emergence of complex biological systems (such
as consciousness), such as, the apparent fine-tuning of evolutionary
development (the anthropic principle), or those that emphasize the
transcendent to explain the 'ultimate realities' of human existence and
our relationship to God.

Enrichment: A role-play of the arguments and counter-arguments
recreating the Scopes 'Monkey Trial' could also be enacted. How has
the debate 'moved on' from those that occurred in Victorian England?

Further reading and resources

Hedley Brooke, J. (1991) *Science and Religion: Some Historical
Perspectives*. Cambridge: Cambridge University Press.

This book is an historical and critical guide to the developing
relationship between scientific thought and religious belief.

Crick, F. (1995) *The Astonishing Hypothesis: The Scientific Search for the
Soul*. New York: Simon & Schuster.

This book is an attempt to apply the methodology of science to
the search for the soul.

The Complete Works of Charles Darwin Online: *http://darwin-
online.org.uk/*

The Darwin Correspondence Project: *http://www.darwinproject.ac.uk/*

A website dedicated to publishing complete transcripts, in chron-
ological order, of all letters written by and to Charles Darwin.

Dawkins, R. (2006) *The Blind Watchmaker*. Harmondsworth: Penguin.

This is the classic, introductory account of the process of evolution by natural selection.

Science and Religion in Schools Project (2006) *Science and Religion in Schools*. Victoria, BC: Trafford Publishing. Topic 4c: Evolution and Creation.

Ward, K. (1996) *God, Chance and Necessity*. Oxford: Oneworld.
The 'new materialism' argues that science and religious belief are incompatible. This book considers such arguments from cosmology, biology, and sociobiology viewpoints, and 'shows that modern scientific knowledge does not undermine belief in God, but points to the existence of God'.

Wilson, E. O. (2001) *The Diversity of Life*. Harmondsworth: Penguin.
This book describes how the species of the world became diverse, and why the threat to this diversity today is beyond the scope of anything we have known before.

Lesson 3: The ills that befall us

Following on from the previous lesson, this lesson examines the philosophical and theological explanations given for the notions of suffering, punishment and illness. The lesson begins with students giving their moral interpretations of ancient and religious stories and then an examination of the theological interpretations of such issues, and the problem for theodicy when accounting for our developing understanding of the natural world and our ability to overcome personal, physical 'decay'.

Key words and phrases

Cleanliness, estrangement, illness, morality, punishment, purity, theodicy.

Key learning objectives

By the end of the lesson all will:

- know that, for many religious adherents, the emergence of conscious human beings is necessary to justify the existence of a Creator God.

By the end of the lesson most will:

- reflect on how, for many religious traditions, human suffering is linked to how we behave spiritually.

By the end of the lesson some will:

- suggest the ways we can alleviate suffering by addressing human beings religious needs.

Concepts

From a religious tradition:

*   suggest how human punishments are the result of moral freedom.

From human experience:

*   reflect on how human beings don't just use physical means to explain illness.

From the study of religion:

*   identify the connection between perceived human immorality and estrangement from God.

Lesson structure

1   Opener: Recount tales of humans misusing knowledge forbidden to them, such as Prometheus. What are the moral readings of such tales? Are there any similar morality tales in the students' lives?

2   *Make impersonal observations of how specific religious principles determine responses to particular issues.* Recall Adam and Eve's punishments for disobeying God. Contrast with evolutionist accounts of humans achieving their 'dominant' position on Earth. How have theologians interpreted the fact that this 'fall' from grace has been replaced by a 'rise' towards moral and rational action? Is this because humanity is intended to know and love God, and to care for the Earth? If humans seek knowledge before they are ready for it, without responsibility, and use it selfishly, does this lead to an estrangement from God?

3   *Enable students to reflect on their emotional response to issues.* Discuss the problems for religious adherents surrounding the notion of *theodicy*. How have religions addressed the task of justifying God in the face of the suffering caused to creatures of all kinds? How have different thinkers explored the notion of evil (*moral*: activities of human beings,

natural: caused to humans by non-human creation – earthquakes, tsunamis – and *evolutionary*: the suffering and futility within the non-human creation as a result of natural selection)? Does non-human creation have any intrinsic value? How can a God that takes delight over creation and design permit mass extinctions? Your discussion might include reference to: John Hick (Evil is necessary to 'soul making'. Human suffering, consequently, contributes to human soul development.), Keith Ward (Evil is necessary for the emergence of a Creation with a consciousness that can 'know' its Creator.) and Ruth Page (Anthropocentrism is a distraction. God is rather a 'creator of possibilities', and keeps company with those possibilities as they unfold.).

4 *Use their personal experiences to engage with specific issues.* Is illness a purely physical phenomenon? Recall the importance of cleanliness and purity (dietary laws in Hinduism, Sikhism, Judaism and Islam) in differing religious traditions (ritual bathing, washing before prayers). Also explore Scriptural passages that focus on illness and disease such as the Ten Plagues, which may be interpreted as a punishment bestowed on those who had become estranged from God.

Examine historical and contemporary religious views of illness and disease (leprosy, plague, Aids; the role of spiritual/faith healers/shamans), and the needs to 'wash away' sins to achieve a moral and spiritual reconnection with the divine (baptism).

Enrichment: Explore other scriptural examples of 'moving away' from God: such as, worship of the golden calf. What moral lessons do such writings explore? Is this the spiritual decay of a community, not just the individual?

Further reading and resources

Bauby, J. –D. (1998) *The Diving-bell and the Butterfly*. New York: Fourth Estate.

This is the memoir of the victim of the rare locked-in syndrome – the only way he could he express himself (and record his thoughts) was by blinking of his left eye.

Fadiman, A. (1998) *The Spirit Catches You and You Fall Down: A Hmong Child, her American Doctors and the Collision of Two Cultures*. New York: Farrar Straus & Giroux Inc.

Hick, J. (2007) *Evil and the God of Love*. London: Palgrave Macmillan.

Page, R. (1996) *God and the Web of Creation*. London: SCM Press.

Sontag, S. (1979) *Illness as Metaphor*. London: Allen Lane.
    This books looks at the metaphors and myths surrounding certain illnesses, especially cancer.

Lesson 4: It's not our problem

This lesson examines both individual and collective notions of responsibility: starting with your students' reflections on their own health, followed by an investigation of the role of spiritual or religious understanding in Western and non-Western medical approaches.

A debate, focusing on the different possible moral responses to our growing awareness of the environmental pressures facing our planet, and an analysis of scriptural texts, both extend this lesson's exploration of religious responses to ethical issues, and makes the link to the next lesson's examination of the philosophical and theological ideas surrounding personal agency.

Key words and phrases

Collective, environmentalism, individualism, intervention, responsibility, stewardship.

Key learning objectives

By the end of the lesson all will:

- know that, for many people, there are real differences between individual and collective responsibilities.

By the end of the lesson most will:

- reflect on the range of different responses that can be given to the same moral question.

By the end of the lesson some will:

- suggest how different religious traditions have influenced the way environmental issues have been addressed.

Concepts

From a religious tradition:

- suggest how scriptural writings may be used as the basis for therapeutic treatments.

From human experience:

- reflect on the origins of different moral positions.

From the study of religion:

- identify the various different ways different religious traditions view the relationship of humanity and the Earth's resources the Earth.

Lesson structure

1 *Enable students to reflect on their emotional response to issues.* Opener: What do your students understand by the term 'responsible adult'? How are our views of our responsibilities, with regards to our own health (smoking, drugs, safe sex), a reflection of individual responsibility and the consequences of our actions?

2 What do religious traditions say? Should medicine be purely mechanistic? What is different about the holistic approaches (www.chisuk.org.uk) of traditional Ayurvedic (www.nchtuk.org) and Chinese (www.rchm.co.uk) 'alternatives' and what are their religious origins?

3 *Use their personal experiences to engage with specific issues.* Morality debate: What individual responsibilities do we each have to take for the environmental state of the planet? Set up groups to argue from a range of different positions. Position no. 1: 'you've got to feel guilty unless your 'green credentials' are impeccable'. Position no. 2: 'What does it matter – we can't do anything about it, and if we do, there's always going to be someone else who won't – so why should I/we lose out'. Position

no. 3: 'Science and technology will solve the 'environmental problem''. Position no. 4: 'If I was poor and had nothing, why should I suffer so that the rich can stay rich'. Position no. 5: 'It's our duty to look after the Earth. It would be morally wrong not to do so'.

4 *Make impersonal observations of how specific religious principles determine responses to particular issues.* Project: Analysis of scriptural writings of different religious traditions (see also www.arcworld.org). How do these reflect the way different nations have reacted to environmental concerns (for example, how does Shintoism's view on the environment reflect the Japanese stance on whaling or, in more general terms, animal rights and environmental ethics)?

Further reading and resources

Berry, R. J. (2003) *God's Book of Works: The Nature and Theology of Nature.* Edinburgh: T & T Clark.

This book argues that the contribution of religious belief to environmental science is highly important, not only in theoretical terms but also in practice.

Orr, D. W. (1994) *Earth in Mind: On Education, Environment, and the Human Prospect.* Washington, DC: Island Press.

'Much of what has gone wrong with the world', this book argues, 'is the result of inadequate and misdirected education that: alienates us from life in the name of human domination' and 'deadens the sense of wonder for the created world'.

Science and Religion in Schools Project (2006) *Science and Religion in Schools.* Victoria, BC: Trafford Publishing. Unit 6: Environmental Issues, Medical Ethics and Animal Rights.

Lesson 5: Free will: who cares?

This lesson develops themes introduced in the previous lesson, and allows your students to explore how religions have tried to make sense of how individuals – and human beings in general – have an impact on the world we live in.

We start with an examination of religious traditions' approaches to assuaging the egocentric tendencies that are prevalent in adolescence, and then how human actions – with particular reference to environmental issues – have been cited, in contrasting philosophical perspectives, as significant or insignificant factors in the ultimate fate of the human species.

This also allows your students to formulate questions for examination in the final session that explores the 'importance' of human beings and religions' reasons for our existence.

Key words and phrases

Agency, deep ecology, fatalism, free will, Gaia, stewardship.

Key learning objectives

By the end of the lesson all will:

- know that, for many people, personal agency is central to having a purpose.

By the end of the lesson most will:

- reflect on the fact that the actions of human beings are not necessarily important to the human race's ultimate survival.

By the end of the lesson some will:

- suggest how religious traditions have countered people's tendency to fatalism.

Concepts

From a religious tradition:

- suggest how prayers and meditation are means to intercede with God and affect our life's course.

From human experience:

- reflect that the independence individuals experience can be explored in fatalistic ways.

From the study of religion:

- identify personal agency with God's action in the world.

Lesson structure

1 Listen and look at the lyrics to the REM song (or similar), 'It's the End of the World as We Know It'. What is wrong in taking a 'superficial' approach to life? Should we not just try and maximize the pleasure and fun? Do we give too great a status to human agency?

2 *Use their personal experiences to engage with specific issues*: Examine the relative importance given to free will in different religious traditions. How have religions responded to nihilist sentiments? Do students think that our current culture is nihilistic? Do they have any personal examples or experiences?

3 *Make impersonal observations of how specific religious principles determine responses to particular issues*: What are different religious responses to fatalism with regards to environmental issues? For example, the religious concept of *stewardship* in the Semitic traditions based on Genesis, or the

Jewish concepts of *yetzer ha-ra* (evil inclination) and *yetzer ha-tov* (good inclination) that following the Kabbalistic concept of *tikkun olam* (lit.: repairing the world). Students could be asked to consider the thesis that Creation caused a disunity in the world and the divine sparks were scattered throughout the universe, and Humanity's task is therefore to repair the world, and, according to Judaism, to bring God's holiness (*kedusha*) into the world.

Contrast with Arne Naess' *Deep Ecology* and James Lovelock's *Gaia Hypothesis* and their conclusions that the importance placed on the contribution of human beings to the Earth's ecology should either be reduced, as it is, in the long term, insignificant.

4 *Enable students to reflect on their emotional response to issues*. Plenary: Are students optimistic, pessimistic or ambivalent about the human race's long-term survival? Do they seek and find comfort, solace or purpose in religious responses? If not, what, if anything, would make them change their opinion?

Enrichment: Other nihilistic accounts could be examined: Book: Turgenev's (1848) *Father & Son*; Television: *Edge of Darkness* (BBC 1982); Film: *Dr. Strangelove* – cartoons and comedy (e.g. Jewish humour).

Further reading and resources

Capra, F. (1997) *The Web of Life: A New Synthesis of Mind and Matter*. London: Flamingo.

This book argues that we are shifting away from a mechanistic to a holistic, ecological world view.

Lovelock, J. (2010) *The Vanishing Face of Gaia: A Final Warning*. Harmondsworth: Penguin.

This book's foci are the terrifying environmental problems that we will confront in the twenty-first century. 'The earth, as it always has done, will save itself. It is up to us to save the human race'.

Naess, A. (2008) *Ecology, Community and Lifestyle: Outline of an Ecosophy*, trans. David Rothenberg. Cambridge: Cambridge University Press.

The basic thesis of this book is that environmental problems are only to be solved by people, and people will be required 'to make value judgements in conflicts that go beyond narrowly conceived human concerns'.

Thoreau, H. D. (1847/1997) *Walden: Or, Life in the Woods*. New York: Dover Books.
The classic, autobiographical account of an experiment in solitary living, and how one person adapted his living to the natural world around him.

Lesson 6: Taking our place in the universe

This final lesson draws on ideas and information your students have focused on in the previous lessons, as it examines one of the issues central to the study of religions, namely the 'purpose' for human existence.

Theistic and dharmic explanations for human existence are the focus for the lesson: eschatological and philosophical explanations are studied, and how these have been represented and portrayed in religious literature and visual imagery.

Key words and phrases

Destiny, eschatology, fulfilment, heaven, purpose.

Key learning objectives

By the end of the lesson all will:

- know that understanding the ultimate purpose of human beings is central to our quest for knowledge and our actions.

By the end of the lesson most will:

- reflect on the way different religious traditions describe how a human being might reach heaven.

By the end of the lesson some will:

- suggest how understanding of the material world has had an impact on Christian eschatological thinking.

Concepts

From a religious tradition:

- suggest how scriptural writings may be read and understood to perceive the destiny of human beings.

From human experience:

- reflect on how humans give themselves a sense of purpose.

From the study of religion:

- identify the various different religious traditions' views on the afterlife.

Lesson structure

1 Opener: Describe a scientific (materialist) account of the probable end of the universe. Ask your students if this is unduly depressing?

2 *Make impersonal observations of how specific religious principles determine responses to particular issues.* Contrast with the theistic viewpoint that human beings are ultimately connected to God, that the human soul is not autonomous and, in the Christian tradition, the resurrection of Jesus is the start of the eschatological transformation (e.g. 1 Corinthians 15.20).

3 *Enable students to reflect on their emotional response to issues.* Ask students if they have an image of heaven? How have they developed that image, from the media, literary or artistic representations, or from scriptural writings?

4 *Use their personal experiences to engage with specific issues.* Examine Judaic ideas of afterlife. Is this similar to an Islamic Paradise or achievement of the Brahmic state of eternal bliss?

Enrichment: Look at human resurrection in the Abrahamic faiths. How have the difficulties of physical resurrection at the Last Judgment been addressed in the interpretation of scriptural writings by Christian theologians such as Paul Tillich or Jurgen Moltmann?

Final plenary: Possible questions to ask your students: Is there a topic or issue that we have explored during the course that you would want to examine in greater detail? What are the ideas, if any, that have made the most sense to you and why?

Further reading and resources

Hick, J. (1985) *Death and Eternal Life*. London: Palgrave Macmillan.

Hick, J. (2006) *The New Frontier of Religion and Science*. London: Palgrave Macmillan.

This book challenges the prevailing naturalistic assumption that 'the mind is, either identical with or, a temporary by-product of brain activity'. It also 'discusses religion as institutions and religion as inner experience of the Transcendent', and suggests a form of spirituality for today.

Peacocke, A. (2001) *Paths from Science Towards God: The End of all our Exploring*. Oxford: Oneworld.

This book argues that the divine principle is at work behind all aspects of existence – both spiritual and physical.

Further reading

Qualifications and Curriculum Authority (2007) *Religious Education Programme of Study (Non-statutory) for Key Stage 4 and Years 12 and 13.* London: QCA.

Sagan, C. (2007) *The Varieties of Scientific Experience: A Personal View of the Search for God.* New York: Penguin.

Scottish Government (2009) *Curriculum for Excellence: Religious and Moral Education.* Edinburgh: Learning & Teaching Scotland.

Ward, K. (2008) *The Big Questions in Science and Religion.* Templeton Foundation Press.
   This book explores ten questions that consider if religious beliefs can survive in the scientific age.

Welsh Assembly Government (2008) *National Exemplar Framework for Religious Education for 3 to 19-year-olds in Wales: Guidance for Local Education Authorities and Agreed Syllabus Conferences.* Cardiff: Curriculum and Assessment Division.

Index